Effective guide to Communication and Speech Making

JUSTIN CHUKWUNONSO NZEKWE

The Art of Oratory

Copyright © 2016

JUSTIN CHUKWUNONSO NZEKWE

Email: justinnzekwe@yahoo.com

First published 2009

Second Published 2016

All rights reserved
No part of this book may be reproduced, stored in retrieval system or transmitted in any form or by any means without the prior written permission of the author, except in the case of brief quotations embodied in critical articles and reviews.

First Published by:
CHIMAVIN PRODUCTIONS LTD.

Second Published by:
VIVIPEDIA PUBLICATIONS

ISBN: 10: 1535272112
ISBN-13: 9781535272117

Justin C. Nzekwe

DEDICATION

I'm
grateful to the
ALMIGHTY GOD
the author of Communication
and to
ALL HUMANITY
at large.

"If your voice is as loud as a trumpet and your story as sweet as honey, but you could not hold the attention of your audience, it is like a sweet melody played in a lonely wilderness with no listener. The speaker should know that the audience is his/her shop and so gaining their attention is like making good sales for the day."

CONTENTS

FORWARD	15-18
INTRODUCTION	19-21
FEATURES OF THE SECOND EDITION	21
ACKNOWLEDGEMENTS	23
CHAPTER ONE	**25**
HOW TO MAKE AN EFFECTIVE COMMUNICATION	25
WHAT IS COMMUNICATION	26
THE COMMUNICATION PROCESS	26
Source	27
Message	27
Channel	27
Receiver	28
Feedback	28
Noise	29
COMMUNICATION COMPETENCE	29
CRITERIA FOR ACCESSING COMMUNICATION COMPETENCE	
Flexibility	30
Commitment	30
Empathy	31
Effectiveness	31
Sensitivity	31
Adeptness	32
MASS COMMUNICATION	32
MEDIATED AND NON-MEDIATED COMMUNICATION	33
Mediated Communication	33
Non-Mediated Communication	34
Types of Non-Mediated Communication	35
Dyadic Communication	36
Small-Group Communication	36
Public Communication	36
UNDERSTANDING PUBLIC SPEAKING	37
CHARACTERISTICS OF A GOOD PUBLIC SPEAKER	38
Integrity	38
Passion	39
Sensitivity	39

The Art of Oratory

Knowledge	40
Skill	40
Audibility	41
BARRIERS TO EFFECTIVE COMMUNICATION	41
Language Barrier	41
Physical Barriers	42
Emotional Barriers	43
Perceptual Barriers	44
Differences in Backgrounds	45
Poor Listening	46
CHAPTER TWO	**47**
ETHICS OF COMMUNICATION	47
PRINCIPLES FOR ETHICAL COMMUNICATION	48
Ethically Sound Intention	49
A Well Prepared Speech	50
Speech Guided with Sincerity	51
Communication should be Proportionate	52
Communication should be Carried Out with Prudence and Respect	53
CHAPTER THREE	**55**
HOW TO PREPARE A SPEECH	55
ELEMENTS OF SPEECH	56
Speaker	56
Audience	56
Message	57
KINDS OF SPEECH	57
Descriptive Form	58
Argumentative Form	60
Expository Form	63
THE PURPOSE OF A SPEECH	64
Speech to Inform	65
Speech to Persuade	66
Speech to Actuate	66
Speech to Entertain	67
Speech to Present	68
Speech to Accept	68
KNOWING AN IDEA WORTH WRITING ABOUT	69
CHOOSING A TOPIC	70
Brainstorming	70
Association of Ideas	71
PLANS & POLICIES	73

PERSONS	73
SOURCES OF SPEECH	74
Magazines and Newspapers	74
Television and Radio	75
Internet	76
Encyclopedia and Dictionaries	76
Books	76
Journals or Periodicals	76
Observation	77
Documentaries/Histories	77
Past Experience	78
Questionnaires	78
Interview	79
HOW YOUR IDEA CAN LEAD YOUR AUDIENCE	80
Begin with a Familiar Idea	80
Have a Sequential Arrangement of Ideas	80
Use a Directional	81
Use Emphasis/Repetition	82
GIVE YOUR SPEECH A STAND OR CONCLUSION	82

CHAPTER FOUR	**83**
HOW TO USE A DILEMMA	83
KINDS OF DILEMMA	83
Simple Constructive Dilemma	84
Complex Constructive Dilemma	84
Complex Destructive Dilemma	85
Simple Destructive Dilemma	85
CONFRONTING THE DILEMMA	85
Taking It by the Horns	86
Escaping Between the Horns	86
Rebuttal	87

CHAPTER FIVE	**91**
MASTERING SPEECH SOUNDS AND TECHNIQUES	91
SPEECH SOUNDS	91
CHARACTERISTIC OF SPEECH	91
PHONETICS AND PHONOLOGY	92
VOWEL	93
CONSONANTS	94
PLACES OF ARTICULATION FOR THE CONSONANTS	95

The Art of Oratory

Bilabials	95
Labiodentals	95
Dentals	95
Alveolars	96
Palatals	96
Velars	96
Glottal	96
ORGAN OF SPEECH	96
Lips	96
Teeth	96
Tongue	97
Uvula	97
Alveolar Ridge	97
Hard Palate	97
Glottis	97
Velum	98
PARTS OF SPEECH	98
NOUN	99
CLASSIFICATION OF NOUNS	99
Proper nouns	99
Common nouns	99
Collective nouns	100
PRONOUN	100
Personal Pronoun	100
Possessive pronoun	100
Reflexive Pronoun	100
Indefinite pronoun	101
Interrogative pronoun	101
VERB	101
Auxiliary verb	101
Regular verb	101
Irregular verbs	102
ADVERB	102
Adverb of Manner	102
Adverb of Time	102
Adverb of Place	102
Adverb of Degree	102
ADJECTIVE	103
PREPOSITION	103
CONJUNCTION	103
Coordinating conjunctions	103
Subordinating conjunction	103
INTERJECTION	104

CHAPTER SIX — 105
HOW TO PRACTICE A SPEECH — 105
    Effort and Commitment — 106
    Learning To Live With Speech Impediments — 106
    Putting a Severe Effort to Improve — 107
    Learning the Proper Way of Imitation — 108
    Practice How to Write — 109
    Practice Memorizing Relevant Things — 109
THE DOS AND DONTS IN PRACTICING YOUR SPEECH — 110

CHAPTER SEVEN — 115
HOW TO MEMORISE YOUR SPEEH — 115
USE OF MNEMONICS — 116
SOME POPULAR MNEMONIC DEVICES — 117
    Method of loci — 117
    Acronym method — 118
    Keyboard Method — 118
INDIVIDUAL DIFFERENCES IN MEMORISING — 118
    Rote Memory — 119
    Meaningful Memory — 119
    Ideational or Logical Memory — 119
    Visual Memory — 119
    Motor Memory — 119
    Laud Memory — 120
    Acoustic Memory — 120
    Number Memory — 120
    Verbal Memory — 120
    Color Memory — 120
    Eidetic Memory — 120
THEORIES OF RETENTION — 121
    Interference Theory — 121
    Decay Theory — 121
    Motivated-Forgetting Theory — 121
    The Displacement Theory — 121
    The Loss Access — 122
    Current Appraisal — 122
THE LAWS OF LEARNING — 122
    The Law of Intensity — 122
    The Law of Organization — 122

	The Law of Contiguity	122
	The Law of Exercise	123
	The Law of Effect	123
	The Laws of Facilitation and of Inference	123
EFFICIENCY LEARNING AND REMEMBERING		123
	Having the Intention to Remember	123
	Whole Learning	124
	Recitation	124
	Distributed Practice	124
	Imitation	125
	Knowledge of Results	125
	Survey	125
	Review	125
	Question	126

CHAPTER EIGHT   127
HOW TO DELIVER YOUR SPEECH   127
NONVERBAL AND VERBAL COMMUNICATION   127
PHYSICAL DELIVERY/NONVERBAL COMMUNICATION 129
    Body Movements   130
    Gestures   130
    Eye Contact   133
    Facial Expressions   134
    Physical Appearance   135
THE USE OF SPACE   137
    Elevation   137
    Distance   137
    Obstructions   138
UNITS AND PROCESSES OF SPEECH   139
    Rate   140
    Volume   141
    Quality and Articulation   142
    Pauses   144
STAGE FRIGHT   144

CHAPTER NINE   147
HOW TO INTRODUCE YOUR SPEECH   147
MAJOR DEVICES FOR WINNING AN AUDIENCE   151
    Humor   151
    Emotion   151
    Novelty   152

Oddity	152
Conflict	152
Sex	153
Intensity	153
Coherency	153
Familiarity	154
Proximity	154
Progress	154
Suspense	155
Religion	155
Economy	155
Health	156
Self-Interest	156
EXAMPLES OF AN INTRODUCTORY SPEECH	156

CHAPTER TEN	**161**
HOW TO UNDERSTAND YOUR AUDIENCE	161
EXTERNAL FACTORS	161
The Population of the Audience	161
Situation	162
Environment	163
INTERNAL FACTORS	164
Sex	164
Cultural and Ethnic Background	165
Social Status	165
Educational Level and Intelligence	166
Attitudes and Beliefs of the Audience	166
Attitude toward Time	167
Attitude to Foreigners	167
TEMPERAMENTAL DISPOSITIONS	168
The Sanguine	168
Choleric	169
Melancholies	169
Phlegmatic	170
DISTINCTIVENESS OF AUDIENCE ACCORDING TO AGE	171
SOCIAL PERCEPTION OF PEOPLE	172
IMPRESSION FORMATION	172
First Impressions	172
Social Schemas	173
Implicit Personality Theory	173
Prototype	174

The Art of Oratory

Stereotypes	174
Impression in Status Transactions	174
MAKING YOUR AUDIENCE FRIENDS	175
Similarity	176
Complementarity	176
Reciprocity	176
Physically Attractiveness	176
Proximity	176
QUALITIES OF FRIENDSHIP	177
Supportiveness	177
Intelligence	177
Sincerity	177
Sense of Humor	177
Affection	178
Willing to Make out Time for Others	178
Good Conversationalist	178
THE PSYCHOLOGY OF THE AUDIENCE	178
Physiological Needs	180
Safety Needs	181
Love and Belonging Needs	181
Esteem Needs	181
Self-Actualization Needs	182

CHAPTER ELEVEN	**186**
HOW TO EFFECTIVELY PERSUADE AN AUDIENCE	186
ETHOS	187
PATHOS	189
VARIOUS TYPES OF EMOTION	190
Anger	190
Fear	190
Shame	191
Pity/Compassion	192
Envy or Jealousy	193
Love	193
THE EMOTIONAL STATE OF THE SPEAKER	195
EVIDENCE	195
VERIFIABLE EVIDENCE	196
AUTHORITATIVE EVIDENCE	197
QUALITIES OF AUTHORITATIVE OPINION	197
Mental Fitness	197
Unprejudiced	197
Must Have Evidence	198

Up-to-date Knowledge	198
Restricted Field of Specialty	198
Sincerity	198
LOGOS	198
INDUCTIVE REASONING	198
Factors that can make Inductive Arguments strong	199
Appeal to authority	199
Appeal to Analogy	199
Appeal to Enumeration	199
DEDUCTIVE REASONING	200
Possible Features of a Valid Deductive Argument	
Possible Features of Invalid Deductive Arguments	
AVOIDANCE OF FALLACIES IN REASONING	201
Appeal to Tradition	202

CHAPTER TWELVE	**205**
HOW TO USE A MICROPHONE	205
TYPES OF MICROPHONE	206
The Lavaliere Microphone	206
Hand Held Microphone	207
The Stationary Microphone	207
HOW TO POSITION A MICROPHONE	208
Distance	208
Phase Problem	209
Proximity Effect	210
GUIDELINES FOR CHOOSING A MICROPHONE	210
MOUNTING A MICROPHONE	211
SOME METHODS OF MOUNTING A MICROPHONE	212
THE BOOM STAND	212
Table Top Stand	213
Shock Absorption	213
KNOWING HOW TO TURN THE MICROPHONE ON AND OFF	
THE NEED FOR A SOUND CHECK	214
THE GENERAL RULES OF MICROPHONE TECHNIQUE	214
MAINTAINANCE OF MICROPHONE	216

CHAPTER THIRTEEN	**219**
HOW TO CONCLUDE YOUR SPEECH	219

SUGGESTED PRECAUTIONS TO BE TAKEN IN CONCLUDING A SPEECH 222
    Climbing up and down the slope 222
    Be content With What You Have 222
    Attempt Summary 222
    Unveiling Your Speech 222
    Humor can be Instrumental 222
    Roundabout a Circle 223
    You Can Apply an Emotion 223
    Give them a challenge 223
    Add Your Opinion 223
    Strike the Middle in Matters of Time 223
    Curtail Excess 224
SOME EXAMPLES OF CONCLUDING SPEECHES 224

APPENDIX **231**
Appendix One 231
David Cameron June 2016

Appendix Two 236
Martin Luther King Jr. 28 August 1963

Appendix Three 242
Unachukwu Nnamdi Cyril, CCE 25 June, 2009

Appendix Four 247
His Holiness Pope Francis 24 September 2015

References **259**

Justin C. Nzekwe

FORWARD

The invitation to write the FORWARD to this book is likened to a request by a suitor to marry a lady. To accept or reject this offer needs an overnight meditation for the following reasons:

(a) Will attention be focused on the substance of form of my write-up?
(b) Will my grammatical exposition make the author laugh at me or with me?

I put it to you, that as an invited guest, I have the privilege to adorn and garnish the author's cake the way I please. This therefore is my embellishment.

The author has highlighted in this book the obvious fact that not all who talk can speak impressively, not all who speak can discuss meaningfully, and not all considered educated are articulate and rhetoric in public speaking. Many are shy and nervous and dread addressing the public, as children fear to walk in darkness.

Certainly, a conversation between a few people differs from a speech to an audience of diverse background, culturally, ethnically or religiously. A state of disaster becomes imminent when a speaker on whom all attention is focused makes a caricature of himself either by any modicum of indiscipline or a quantum of ignorance of the issue in discussion. When the speaker does not have the ability or the capacity to deal with the barriers to effective communication, these barriers graduate into an insurmountable chasm. The exercise then becomes a failure. In the art of oratory, a failure emanating from lack of diligence on the part or the speaker equates to self immolation.

The author frowns at unethical communication such as was applied by Adolf Hitler and Iddi Amin Dada who had no respect for public policy, morality, sincerity and decorum, thus, throwing their countries and the world into a state of political and social delirium.

I agree with the writer for elucidating the "sine-qua-non" of all speeches, thus, the speaker, the message to be transmitted, the audience; and the occasions when speeches became imperative.

Just as any reasonable man has a reason for his conduct so also every speech must have a purpose and the author lists the *decideratum* of every speech. There must be a correspondence between the speaker's ideas and his address and these ideas can be got from various sources.

Speakers of Greek era developed the oratoric tactics of dilemma which may be simple or complex. A dilemma is posed by the speaker who also suggests an escape route to persuade his audience to accept his suggestion so as to achieve the purpose of his speech. This art is manipulated by radicals, fundamentalists, rascals, vandals and leaders of military *coup-de tat*.

The author dives into how to prepare and deliver speeches, the art of imitation, speed reading, and memorizing, use of mnemonics and the laws of learning. He advises that every speaker ought to communicate with his audience not only verbally but also nonverbally. This involves gestures, or body motions, eye-contacts, facial expressions, mode of dress and physical appearances. The quality of a speech is assessed by its rate of delivery or speed of speaking, the pitch and volume of the voice as well as its quality and the speaker's articulation, phonetics and pauses.

Like an academic thesis or dissertation, which has an introduction, a summery and conclusion; a homily which has a prologue and epilogue; a musical operatic demonstration which has an overture and a development, so also every ideal speech must have an introduction, a summary and a conclusion. The introduction wets the appetite of the audience, while the summary and conclusion make the principal message-content stick into the memory.

A speaker must know the psychological disposition of the audience so as to keep up their interest, and be selective in his language so as not to irritate the sensitivity of the people. Similarly, the temperament, and age of the audience must be taken into consideration because the people are isolated when a speech or topic designed for adults is delivered to children. A speaker who makes the people laugh gets a prolonged ovation.

According to the author, the success of a speech is "winning the audience", and persuading the people to accept your line of reasoning on an issue. This is accomplished by the major means of persuasion: ethos, pathos, evidence and logos.

The writer is so comprehensive in his topic-approach that he even elaborates on how to use the microphone, a device with its accessories, the amplifiers and speakers, invented in 1907 by Dr. Lee Deforest. The most fascinating brand is the Lavaliere microphone, which allows the speaker to move or walk around freely with his hands free to perform gestures.

This type of microphone is clipped to the speaker's dress, coat or tie. While gospel preaches and judges prefer the stationary microphones, musicians, actors and I admire the hand-held models.

I agree with the author for saying that in conclusion, the speaker knits his entire message content into a specific and rememberable whole. This in the legal profession, is equivalent to the lawyer's submission, by which he persuades the judge to accept his point of view on the issue in dispute, considering the evidence adduced.

Finally, the author ends the work by reference to famous speeches made by international personalities. This is in conformity with the theory of history, that history of every age is the story of men and women who by their actions influenced the people of that age and the world at large.

It is my contention that this book written in classical English is a vindication of the academic and theological excellence of the Seat of Wisdom Seminary and School of Journalism that nurtured the author.

'The Art of Oratory', is simply the crown of every library, for it constitutes the *primus inter pares* among books relied upon by men of oratoric splendor, lawyers, men of God, and leaders of thought among others. Read it!

BARRISTER PROF. J.O.L. EZEALA.
Dean, Faculty of Law,
Madonna University, Okija,
Anambra State.

INTRODUCTION

The book you are holding in your hands is special in the sense of the special role it is going to play in your life and for humanity. Holding it has already made you special because you have the prospect of gaining that greatest power controlled by great men and women in history-oratory.

All men are powerful, but some are more powerful than others: they are those who possess the rare power of oratory. Many have good ideas and sound voices, but have the greatest impediment of all, which is language. A copybook written 3000 years ago found on Pharaoh's tomb was said to contain a write-up, "make thyself a craftsman in speech for thereby thou shall gain the upper hand. The tongue of man is his weapon and speech is mightier than fighting." The greatest revolutionary movement in history can only be traced back to an orator – it is only an orator who has the magic power of molding, remolding and demolding histories, ideologies, events and any other extraordinary thing in the sand of existence.

Every history has gotten her ration of people who have acquired this treasure – oratory. History can never forget people like Archbishop Fulton Sheen, Martin Luther King, Jr., Frankline Roosevelt, Elizabeth Dole, Margaret Thatcher, Adolf Hitler, Nelson Mandela, Nnamdi Azikiwe and others, whose power of oratory have remolded either positively or negatively the different parts of the world they existed in

The Art of Oratory

their time. This you can do even more than they once did. Like a porter, you have acquired the art of molding. The power to shape is simply in your hands as you read this book.

THE ART OF ORATORY is special and egg-like. It is special, in the sense of its special role in your history, and it is egg-like in the sense that when you use it well, it is going to serve as nourishment to your intellectual curiosity, and as an invigorator which renews your strength. If mishandled, it might fall off your hand and become useless because of its fragile nature. The fact that you are holding it had already made you special and that you have opened it, had started nourishment in you. It is going to open up your eyes to see the greatest treasure on your door post and your mouth to control and profess the power and wonders of nature. To your shyness, it will also consign to oblivion: your speech impediments, your inarticulateness and you will be transformed into a new you.

For those who ask, what's my connection with oratory? "Am not going to be the president, preacher neither am I going to lead any cause", we promise you that the day is coming when you will need it, maybe in the family or elsewhere, for life is unpredictable. Further, do not forget that the need to be a good speaker is limitless, "the importance of such skill is true across the board – for accountants and architects, teachers and technicians, scientist and stockbrokers. Even in highly specialized fields such as civil and mechanical engineering, employers consistently rank the ability to communicate above technical knowledge when deciding whom to hire and whom to promote?" So, nobody is exempt 'when young or old from this noble art, because it is never too late to change the world. If you are still young, start now when the road is still clear and simple, if old, grab it as if that is the only thing remaining in your life to make it fulfilled.

The book you are still holding addresses so many topical issues and stresses so many *organum* (tool) you need in order to achieve all the best you need to achieve in oratory and communication in general. We firmly promise you that this book will take you by the hand and repair you and make you conquer your weakness in the area of public speaking and communication in general. Keep a date with us and read on to discover more on the next page of this book.

FEATURES OF THE SECOND EDITION

In this second edition of The Art of Oratory, we have tried to diversify our ideas by tracing speech down to its rudiment. We have also updated on what we have with regards to public speaking in order to meet up with the modern challenges. This edition also is a *big bang* in the area of public speaking and communication at large. It is channeled to be useful to students of Mass Communication, English, Law, Political Science, Philosophy and other disciplines. It is also targeted to be a *vademecum* for every human being regardless of age, race, profession and interest. It is written with everyday English and garnished with some literary skills to make it reader friendly, and easy to digest.

The Art of Oratory

ACKNOWLEDGEMENTS

We are indebted to the people who contributed in one way or another to the success of the first edition of this work. Your efforts and contribution can never be forgotten. I am grateful to the Blessed Trinity and to our Mother Mary with respect to this work. I thank my bishop, Most Rev. Augustine Ukwuoma, and my bishop emeritus, Most Rev. G. O. Ochiagha for their fatherly roles and encouragements. I will never forget my lovely immediate family members, for playing a key role in the publication of this work, and to all Nzekwe's family. I must thank Barr. Prof. J. O. L Ezeala (A Professor of Law), Miss Jane (Lecturer in Mass Com.) Miss Ojiaku E. (Lecturer in Mass Com.) and Frs. Okparaeke P., Elelleh C., Konye M., Akuchie R., and Unadike C., for the able role they played in this work. I also hold in gratitude the efforts of these erudite scholars who proofread this work, Frs., Anagwo C., Obioha P., Dike S., Ohajiekwu C., Ogbu C., Ukoha C., Ogudo K., Ejiofor V., Nwanyanwu D., Mgbeojirikwe K., Nkemjika U., and Mr. Ezechukwu C. You are indeed wonderful. I thank friends and well wishers of whom for want of space, their name did not appear in this work, God is your reward. I thanked the litany of authors whose works were resourceful in the course of this book project, I duff my cap. Above all, I am indebted to the members of *Trinitarian Set, Potential Leaders Forum* and *Catholic For Life* group. I do accept all shortcomings associated with the content of this work, and I pledge to keep updating the work till it attends the perfection of heavens. God bless you all!!!

The Art of Oratory

CHAPTER ONE

HOW TO MAKE AN EFFECTIVE COMMUNICATION

Communication is an integral part of every human being. Lower animals tend to communicate in their own crude way, but human being is the only created being that possesses the maximum potentiality to communicate with his fellow being. Human being communicates through various media and yet comprehension is achieved.

Thus human being is an intersubjective being, a being of dialogue, capable of entering into a relation with his fellow being. Communication through its intersubjective nature helps man to benefit from the perceptions and inferences of others, and increases his knowledge beyond what can be achieved in loneliness and solipsism. Human being can reason abstractly, agree, deny, argue, discuss, manipulate, deceive, display wit, seduce, and maintain an effective social relationships through language.

One of the primary aims of language is to communicate that which is intelligible in a comprehensible manner. Hence Igboanusi maintains that "to communicate is to take a first-person standpoint. It is to posit oneself in relation to others in the world, to declare one's preferences and objectives. The meaning of communication is sociality and communion. Language is geared towards achieving that ultimate communion and understanding by which perfect bonds are built among people in society and eventually among nations."[1]

WHAT IS COMMUNICATION?

Communication for an ordinary person is the process by which information is exchanged through either words or symbols between individuals. But we do not communicate mere words or symbols alone, we also communicate our being or personness, our attitude or behaviour, values, ideas, symbols, etc. Communication therefore, is "the act of transmitting, transferring or exchanging information between individuals through accepted system of signs or symbols, words or behaviour."[2] It is a partial transfer of our being to another being. This transferring of our being is partial because of the unavoidable barriers in the communication processes.

THE COMMUNICATION PROCESS

There are so many elements at work in every communication. These elements are what help us to understand what goes on during communications. These elements are: Source, Message, Channel, Receiver, Decoding and Feedback. However, recent researchers on communication process have also added Noise as one of the processes.

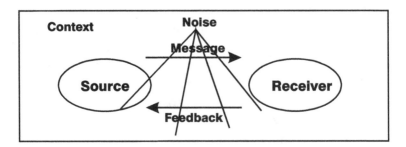

Fig. 1. 1: Graphic representation of communication process.

Source: This is the sender or the originator of a message. The source begins with the thinking out of the message, and organizing of the ideas that would be communicated. This process determines a lot in the quality of materials that are going to be communicated. When the source is not wonderful, the message would hardly be. This is the stage where the message is encoded, and therefore, the sender makes use of symbols – words, visual aids, graphics – to pass the message and produce the required response.

Message: This is the central idea that the source wants to communicate to another person or group of persons. It is very necessary as a speaker to make your message make the right meaning to your audience. Meaning in this context as J. Maurus puts it would imply "the significance which the communicator assigns to feelings and ideas, to objects, persons and events in his environment."[3] Often, the message we intend to pass might not be the message received. This is usually the case when there is not enough synchronization of the verbal message with the nonverbal message. For a better communication, the idea should be clear and distinct and communicated meticulously with appropriate gestures.

Channel: This is the means by which a message is communicated. It is the mode by which a message moves from the source to the receiver of the message. The major channels of communication are the light waves and sound waves. This could be narrowed down into the sense organs; eyes, ears, nose, mouth, body etc. However, in most cases, more than one channel can be used to send a message. And as Oberg would have it, "the accuracy with which the message is received increases when more channels are used."[4] This is the reason why face-to-face communication elicits greater understanding than messages communicated over the telephone, radio, and television.

Receiver: This is the listener or the audience who hears the message. The receiver decodes the message from the source and put them in a code that he or she can use. The presence of a receiver makes communication possible. Hence, Lucas argues thus: "everything a speaker says is filtered through a listener's *frame of reference* – the total of his or her knowledge, experience, goals, values, and attitudes. Because a speaker and a listener are different people, they can never have exactly the same frame of reference. And because a listener's frame of reference can never be exactly the same as a speaker's, the meaning of a message will never be exactly the same to a listener as to a speaker."[5] This is why great speakers are often audience-centered, and make every frantic effort to blend the different frames of reference of their audience, in order to make sure that a good comprehension of the message is achieved.

Feedback: This is the verbal and nonverbal reactions of the receiver to the source's message. Communication is usually a two-end process, just as the message of the speaker is important, so as the response and the reactions of the audience are also important. However, the reactions of the audience often vary based on the medium of communication. The reaction in an interpersonal communication is quite different from that of a radio speaker or a public speaker. As a public speaker, one should be able to ask himself these questions: "Do your listeners lean forward in their seats, as if paying close attention? Do they applaud in approval? Do they laugh at your jokes? Do they have quizzical looks on their faces? Do they shuffle their feet and gaze at the clock? The message sent by these reactions could be "I am fascinated," "I am bored," "I agree with you," "I don't agree with you," or any number of others."[6] A speaker should know that the message he is passing across is as important as the reaction of the audience with regards to the message. Try as much as possible to adjust your message from time to time in such a way that you get a positive feedback without losing the main kernel of your message.

Noise: This is anything that posses as a hindrance to the message. It is any interference in the encoding and decoding processes that reduces the clarity of a message.[7] This noise can be physical when it has to do with external distractions. It can be mental or psychological when you lack the proper disposition of the mind. It can also be semantic when perception of symbols by a receiver differs from that of the speaker. Noise therefore is an active enemy of effective communication.

COMMUNICATION COMPETENCE
It is obvious that all human beings by nature are capable of communicating. But some communicate more effectively than others. The level of competence differs depending on various factors and orientations. Some people at the early part of their life are competent communicators, but due to lack of further development, they become stunted and remain on that level. While some others who were not competent initially, might through serious practices develop better and become more competent than they used to be.

Communication competence is the ability to send messages which promote attainment of goals while maintaining social acceptability. Competent communicators attempt to align themselves with each other's goals and methods in order to produce a smooth, productive and often enjoyable dialogue.[8] What makes a person competent is the ability to communicate with others with much clarity and distinctness, effectiveness, expertise, coherency, accuracy, comprehensiveness, etc.

CRITERIA FOR ACCESSING COMMUNICATION COMPETENCE

There are many criteria for assessing the competency of communication. But for more clarity, we are going to challenge ourselves here with the major ones among others. They include:

Flexibility (Adaptability):
This is a major criterion for assessing competency in communication. Flexibility involves the ability to work on behaviour and goals to meet the challenges of interactions by choosing the adequate response which increases the possibilities of attaining mutual goals. For Lane, flexibility comprises six factors:[9]

- Social Experience: refers to the participation in various social interactions.
- Social Composure: refers to keeping calm through accurate perception.
- Social Confirmation: refers to acknowledgement of partner's goals.
- Appropriate Disclosure: refers to being sensitive to amount and type of information.
- Articulation: refers to the ability to express ideas through language.
- Wit: refers to the ability to use humour in adapting to social situations; ease tensions.

Commitment:
This involves the ability to get a satisfying result from communication, by trying to put the interest of the other person at heart in order to make a good relationship. In other words, it is a synthesis of one's own needs and perspective with that of others in order to produce mutual acceptance. Lack of confidence in others is a serious problem that can reduce our competence in communication; it makes it

difficult for us to convince others by weakening our relationship with them.

Empathy:
You ought to have some basic knowledge about the other person and be ever ready and disposed to accept the person. Such knowledge will help you know why he or she is behaving the way he/she is behaving. Being empathetic, means the ability to see things from another person's perspective while reasoning in line with emotions of such perspective. Hence, this does not necessarily mean helping the other person; rather it helps the person to accept you, just as you have accepted him/her.

Effectiveness:
This is also a major criterion for assessing competency in communication. An ineffective communicator is not competent. Each communicator has personal goals to achieve through communication. The ability to achieve such personal goals and the objectivity of conversation make one a competent communicator.

Sensitivity:
A good communicator is someone who will always, like chameleon, change to adapt to the nature of every environment. You should be able to avoid overgeneralization because the fact that a method worked out fine in one situation does not necessarily mean that the same method must always work in every situation. Try to discern when you are making sense and when you are no longer making sense. If you feel that you are no longer making any impact, try another method to adapt to the current situation.

Adeptness:
This relates to the ability to be skilful in matters of communication. The ability to learn how to skilfully organize our speech, and being able to use those skills spontaneously makes our message natural, attractive and also makes us competent communicators. "Timing, word-choices, emphasis, inflection, and rhythm must all be integrated in a comfortable and spontaneous way if the skill is to be accepted as it is intended. A message will call motives into question if it seems too awkward and contrived, on the one hand, or so smooth, on the other, that it looks pre-planned."[10] However, communication that is not adept can hardly be seen as competent.

MASS COMMUNICATION

This is the transmission of information to a dispersed, diversified and large number of people through the mass media. It is the process of understanding and sharing meaning through mediated messages to a potentially large audience. The information moves from a single source down to larger number of receivers. However, "what sets mass communication apart is the complexity of the process; the rules and conventions involved in understanding the communication product; the way shared experiences are created for a "mass" audience; and the interpretation of the meanings in a system virtually devoid of feedback."[11] But with the introduction of call back through the radio and television programs, and the introduction of comment box on information posted on the internet, many changes are gradually coming into the perception of mass communication with relation to feedback. The channels of mass communication are: news reports, books, movies, television programs, music videos, advertisements, and articles on internet, magazines and newspapers.

MEDIATED AND NON-MEDIATED COMMUNICATION

Communication can either be mediated or non-mediated. It is mediated when the communication is indirect, when it is not a face-to-face communication. Mediated communication is done through a medium which can either be a television, radio, film, print etc. while the non-mediated communication is direct or a face-to-face encounter between the speaker and the audience.

Mediated Communication:
Mediated communication is a common communication associated with the modern man. Its nature delimits it form attaining the full goal of communication. It is an indirect communication where the source is far removed from the receiver. There is a big gap in space and time from the moment the message is communicated till the time it reaches its targeted audience. This makes it subject to misinterpretation. Think of a Nigerian in 2008, who has never been to America before nor has ever studied about Americans, but is found listening to a 1920 speech recorded as a film in America. You can always imagine the gap and indirect nature of such communication, and you will understand why it would be difficult for such a Nigerian to interpret such a message accurately.

Feedback is one of the major problems of mediated communication. Litfin added that, in mediated communication, the receiver often has no chance to ask questions or to feed back a response to the source. And even if the receiver does, the response is usually indirect. In other words, the feedback itself usually mediated, if in fact it is possible at all.[12] By this statement, Litfin tries to puncture the difficulty that is associated with receiving feedback in mediated communication, where feedback is almost impossible. On the other way round, mediated communications is very important because of its ability to preserve antiquities; through mediated communication, one can now record the voices of dear ones or writings of some geniuses can now be documented and reproduced when needed for the purpose of posterity. In most cases, the target of mediated communication is for a greater number of audiences both within and outside the environment of the speaker or writer.

Non-Mediated Communication:
This is a more direct communication; a face-to-face contact between the communicator and the listener. There is no intermediary between the speaker and the receiver, and the message from non-mediated communication has little chances of error and misinterpretation. The speech is carefully tailored to suit the particular audience. It is a much more efficient communication since the feedback from the message is received immediately or even spontaneously. Think of a speaker who after delivering his speech received applause from his audience or one who received a cold cap, it directly shows the effectiveness of the speech. Think as of a speech that was followed up by questions, such speech directly assures both the speaker and listener the level of understanding and convictions from the speech.

Communication specialists have also observed that the use of microphone is not seen as a medium, rather its purpose is to make the communicated message effective. So, even with the use of microphone, the speaker and receiver will still operate spontaneously within a particular space time. The efficiency of this method of communication through its direct means of operation, and the relationship between the message and the receiver makes it more preferable than mediated means. Once any message is recorded or documented and reproduced some other time, it ceases to be non-mediated, instead it becomes mediated.

Distance in non-mediated communication is not taken arbitrary; it varies depending on occasions and cultures. Some cultures have norms that determine and guide the distance within interpersonal communication, while common sense makes us know that the distance of people communicating in an interview situation should vary from that of friends engaged in a casual chat. Most suitably, Hall identified four suitable distances that might occur in an interpersonal communication event. These are:[13]

1. *Intimate distance:*
    a) Close phase – distance of love making, wrestling comforting or protecting;
    b) Far phase – 6 to 8 inches, hands can reach and grasp extremities of the other person;
2. *Personal distance:*
    a) Close phase 1 ½ to 2 ½ feet, one can hold or grasp the other person;
    b) Far phase 2 ½ to 4 feet, keeping somebody at arm's length;
3. *Social distance:*
    a) Close phase – 4 to 7 feet, impersonal business occurs at this distance;
    b) Far phase 7 to 12 feet;
4. *Public distance:* this is any distance in interpersonal communication beyond 12 feet.

Types of Non-Mediated Communication:
Generally, non-mediated communication is direct, interpersonal and a kind of unaided means of communication. It is the most common and pervasive mode of communication and it is also most suitable for public

speaking. It is divided into three major types: the dyadic, small-group, and public communication.

Dyadic Communication:
When we talk of a dyad; we mean a group of two. Dyadic communication usually comes to play in the form of interview or conversations with the next person. In dyadic communication, communicators can get to know each other intimately. However, because it is immediate and spontaneous, the quality of the feedback is high and the roles of the speaker and listener are freely exchanged.

Small-Group Communication:
A small group is a group with no less than three members and not more than twenty members. If the number reduces to two, it ceases to be a small group and turns to a dyad. When it is greater than twenty members, it prevents the group member's ability to communicate with every member of the group and also ceases to be a small group.

Small group communication is a more complex setting, where communication becomes more complex and complicated. Since the communication is no longer one on one, the distance increases while the intimacy decreases. A lot of things creep in; like the need to reason for the common good instead of personal interest, since more than one person is involved.

Public Communication:
This is much more complex setting that amounts to a limitless number of audiences. The nature of public communication creates an avenue for a lot of people to participate in it with a lesser intimacy among participants. It is very difficult to meet with all the needs of the audience, since the audience acts as the receivers, while the speaker alone acts as the source. It is then difficult to receive the

whole feedbacks from the message transmitted. This means that there is need for a higher level of sensitivity on the part of the speaker in order to enable him adapt to the compelling needs of the audience.

The distance between the speaker and the audience in public communication increases. This reduces the normal intimacy and interaction and therefore increases anxiety in most audience. Herein lies the major cause of stage fright; shivering, fidgeting, dry tongue, speechlessness at the face of audience and other signs associated with tensed speakers.

Furthermore, even though the orator in any form of communication can always display his skills and eloquence, public communication is the major area that differentiates an orator and gives him the more avenues to display his skills and talents. Every aspect of communication matters a lot for the orator, for *no communication, no oratory*; therefore an orator should know his techniques wherever he finds himself.

UNDERSTANDING PUBLIC SPEAKING

When we talk of public speaking, we are looking at communication from the point of view of its formality, structure, and setting. This kind of communication in most cases are geared towards persuading, informing, entertaining, to actuate, accept, present and similar agendas. Public speaking therefore "is the process of understanding and sharing meaning with an audience: one person is generally identified as the source (speaker) and others are recognized as receivers (listeners). The speaker adapts the message to the audience in an attempt to achieve maximum understanding."[14] This is different from other context of communication. It is tailored towards the public, or masses, with the "purpose of delivering a prepared message, speech, lecture or holding a rally or political campaign. The speaker could use public address system, over-head projector (OHP), slides, flip charts, or the audio-visuals for effectiveness."[15] All these ways of enhancing understanding during public speaking, do not guarantee a perfect assimilation of the message communicated. Feedback is sometimes very difficult because of the structure of this context of communication, and in most cases, it is determined by the level of attention given by the audience and by spontaneous outburst of applauds.

Characteristics of a Good Public Speaker
A good speaker is not just a person who make people laugh, or who has a very loud voice that can be heard. Every profession has some ethics guiding it; some demands must be met before one is said to be a professional in any field of life. There are certain characteristics that must be found in every good public speaker. Most of these characteristics are:

1. Integrity
2. Passion
3. Sensitivity
4. Knowledge
5. Skill
6. Audibility

Integrity
The goal of public speaking is not just to win, to achieve whatever you want to achieve regardless of the means, the goal of public speaking is to achieve the goal of your speech with the right intention and the right means. Speakers over

the years have been judged with the measure of goodness possessed by the speaker. The great Roman teacher of rhetoric, Quintilian described an orator (speaker) in Marcus Cato's language, "he must possess the quality which Cato places first and which is in the very nature of things the greatest and most important, that is, he must be a good man."[16] No matter the fame a speaker feels he had achieved and the heights attained. If a speaker has no integrity, it is no more than an empty gong and an ill to humanity.

Passion
When the speaker lacks passion, it simply has a negative impact on the speech and on the speaker. Passion guides you to burn extra oil in order to make your speech good. It is passion that makes you to bring out the best in you and so improve yourself on a regular basis in the art of communicating well. Passion reflects in your voice when you speak, it is not the same thing as shouting. When you speak with an invisible passion in your voice, everybody wants to listen. It also makes sure nobody sleeps or is left out till the end of the speech. Passion can also be seen in your gestures and your appearances during speech. Passion tells your audience that you are convinced of what you are saying and it is true. A speaker that lacks passion is a boring speaker who lacks the vital requirement for his or her profession. He is simply a bad speaker.

Sensitivity
This is an unavoidable quality of every good speaker. A speaker should be able to think with caution and affection inside his audience box. He should be able to place himself in the life situation of his audience and be an objective judge of himself. Hence, a willingness to be sensitive to others stems from a fundamental conviction of their worth. Those who do not value others have few reservations about and experience

little difficulty in manipulating them.[17] It is when you are sensitive that you can guide your audience to the right direction instead of misleading them with lies. Sensitivity also helps you to know when your audience is enjoying your speech, when you are making impact on them and when they are fed up with whatever you are saying. Sensitivity makes you a balanced speaker.

Knowledge

Every speaker must be knowledgeable. No good speaker can speak without having sufficient knowledge of the area he or she wants to dwell in the speech. A speaker should be able to know more on the issue he is speaking about, more than his audience. This can only be possible through proper homework and researches. Versatile speakers are great speakers. A speaker with every other characteristic we have mentioned but lacks the adequate knowledge of the issue he/she is addressing can only qualify to be a jester.

Skill

Public speaking is an art, and therefore requires some level of skill in order to be effective in the field. Many people are very intelligent, have good ideas, capable of researching a topic and digging it to its root, but they end up boring speakers. This is because they don't have the necessary skill. Every other characteristic of public speaking is relevant, but if you possess them all, and yet have no skill to use them, one automatically ends up a failure. One who wants to be a good speaker should have the rudiments of speaking at the finger tips and produce them with ease action. Many people are disposed to some of the skills of oratory by nature, yet practice is the most effective way of acquiring this skill.

Audibility

This is a veritable tool in public speaking. The ability of a speaker to speak loudly points to the credibility of his message. One of the famous philosophers of Language, Wittgenstein in his first publication says, "What can be said at all can be said clearly, and what we cannot talk about we must pass over in silence"[18] It would be of no value delving into an area you do not know, and thereby shying away from making it audible that it may not be understood. We should say what we are sure and say it loud to prove our conviction. The key to this is to always observe your audience to know whether they are following you, or to seek an immediate feedback to know whether they are hearing you. Make sure the sound system is at good shape and make sure you raise your voice so as to be heard.

BARRIERS TO EFFECTIVE COMMUNICATION

Barriers in communication are unavoidable just like an airborne disease, which is usually unavoidable, in as much as one breathes air. We experience a lot of barriers in the process of communicating with others. This is because the meanings we communicate exist only in our mind and that of our receiver, not in the message itself. For effective understanding, there is the need for the speaker and receiver to share a common mental picture, and also the need for a mental alertness and adequate attention from the audience or listener. However, all these requirements are very difficult to be achieved perfectly and therefore barrier are inevitable. Here are some of the popular barriers to communication:

Language Barrier:

The nature of language makes it sometimes to be a barrier to communication. Often in communication, the source encodes the message before transmitting it to the receiver who decodes it. The process of decoding brings a lot of errors due to cultural differences, misinterpretation of symbols and the difficulties of achieving a completely shared meaning. Hence, "of approximately 750,000 words in the English language only about 50,000 (one-fifth) have meanings that have been established and documented that is, their meaning has been frozen so that the word means today what it did year ago.... This small group of words comprises legal and scientific terms, which are purposely precise."[19]

The problem of decoding and lack of shared meaning calls for the speaker to use languages that are more accurate, specific, and can describe by presenting observable facts, events and circumstances. This is to avoid the barriers caused by inappropriate use of words, and the use of ambiguous words which often are beyond the comprehension of the audience.

Language barrier can be observed with the example given by Eric Garner out of the experience of cold war. He said: one of the more chilling memories of the cold war was the threat by the Soviet leader, Nikita Khruschev, saying to the Americans at the United Nations: "We will bury you!" This was taken to mean a threat of nuclear annihilation.

A more accurate reading of Khruschev's words, Garner says, would have been: "We will overtake you!" meaning economic superiority. It was not just language but the fear and suspicion that the West had of the Soviet Union that led to the more alarmist and sinister interpretation."[20] As a speaker, one of the major barriers that can destroy your speech is that of language, use simple words and meanings and avoid ambiguities as much as you can.

Physical Barriers:
This refers to the hindrances of communication experienced within our environments. The nature of the environment or

what goes abnormally within the environment can constitute a big barrier to an effective communication.

In a much compacted environment or hot environment, the audience often finds it difficult to pay attention to the speaker because such an environment breeds distraction. But moderate spacing enhances communication and helps people to relate well with others.

Obstruction also is a major problem here, anything that hinders the audience from seeing the speaker clearly is a barrier. This may come from the nature or arrangement of the hall, the arrangement of technical equipment like; loud speakers, lack of adequate light etc. However, the audience abhors anything that stresses them when listening.

The proximity – the distance between the speaker and the audience can be of a negative impact. When the distance is much, it makes the audience see the speaker as a foreigner talking on his own, they therefore feel less concerned about him after sometime, but when the speaker is closer, the audience sees him as a friend that deserves respect and attention. Hence, physical barriers are rampant among many naïve orators and they impede effective communication.

Emotional Barriers:
This barrier sometimes is associated with the type of person the speaker is, the moral status and his relationship with the subject he is treating. When we see a kind of contradiction in this relationship, we tend to be sceptical because of our emotions and sentiments. "Emotions play a very big part in our acceptance or denial of a message given to us. It may threaten us, make us feel good, make us feel guilty, make us feel happy, make us feel sad."[21]

The emotional state of the speaker and the disposition of the audience have a very big role to play, but more especially the speaker's emotion. If the speaker fails to respect the emotions of the audience through his choice of words he is invariably creating a barrier, or if the speaker is not well disposed, he is likely to end up communicating something different from what he aims at achieving. Hence lack of good emotion disposition is a barrier to communication.

Perceptual Barriers:
Every human being perceives things in his own unique way depending on the factors that influenced his/her life, as well as other natural dispositions. The variety in our perception creates the need to communicate. When everybody is thinking the same thing, there will be no need to communicate any other thing because nothing appears new and interesting again to the other.

In the words of Martin Hahn, "the world constantly bombards us with information: sights, sounds, scents and so on. Our minds organize this stream of sensation into a mental map that represents our perception or reality. In no case is the perception of a certain person the same as the world itself, and no two maps are identical. As you view the world, your mind absorbs your experiences in a unique and personal way. Since your perceptions are unique, the ideas you want to express would differ from other people's even when two people have experienced the same event, their mental images of that event will not be identical."[22] Hence, the uniqueness of our perception is the major source of barrier, because we hardly transfer everything to others exactly the way we perceive them.

Most speakers are too dogmatic that they only speak of those things they think are important and interesting without knowing that those things suit their desire uniquely without necessarily matching with the desire of their audience. The audience also make use of what a German philosopher Immanuel Kant calls "the categories of the mind" or the existing patterns of their mind in order to judge whatever the speaker says. If it fits into their categories, they accept them, but where it doesn't fit in, they are tempted to distort the message. Perception then generally brings a lot of barriers both on the part of the speaker and that of the audience during communication.

Differences in Backgrounds:
The background covers a wide array of information about people, their gender, cultural background, age, education, social status, religion, economic position, political belief, health, temperament, to mention but a few. All these backgrounds play an active role in the information we receive and are liable to become barriers to our communication.

Culturally speaking, people of the same culture have the same behavioural pattern. This is because every culture has a behaviour associated with it, and people in that culture try to appreciate and reward anybody behaving in conformity with their culture more than a foreigner to the culture. Barriers occur here when the speaker imposes his culture on others and when people view and vet the speaker's speech in relation to his affiliation to their culture.

Speaking on educational basis, the educational levels and fields differ, there are people in the scientific circles and those studying arts; there are also the graduates and the non graduates, this is a big barrier to communication since these sets of people view things differently.

Generally, the barriers that are constituted by the differences in background come as a result of the speaker trying, in one way or another, to impose his background on the audience and also the audience trying to make the speaker's speech fit into their background before they can accept it.

Poor Listening:
This barrier emerges from the side of the audience when they fail to listen well. Once we are distracted by anything or once our minds or interests are not in what the speaker is saying, barriers are likely to creep in. Martin Hahn tends to analyse this problem when he said that, "we all let our minds wonder now and then, regardless of how hard we try to concentrate. People are essentially likely to drift off when they are forced to listen to information that is difficult to understand or that has little direct bearing on their own lives. Too few of us simply do not listen well!"[23] It is true that it is difficult to listen for a long time without being distracted, but we should also make an honest effort to avoid distractions as much as we can. We should avoid jumping into conclusions, hasty assumptions and over generalization before the speaker's conclusion and decisions. Try also to read meaning into what you hear in the line of the speaker if you want to avoid this barrier.

A barrier can also come from the speaker when he fails to listen in order to comprehend what the audience has in mind about the subject under discussion. In such a situation, the speaker continues to speak without communicating.

CHAPTER TWO

ETHICS OF COMMUNICATION

Ethics is an imperative to any rational being from conception to death. Ethics is a branch of philosophy that formulates principles and actions that should guide human conduct. It is a lamp that guides us to know the "ought' as good and to do it and to avoid the "ought not" as bad and not worth doing in order to live peacefully within the human community.

Ethics deals with such questions as – what is the good life for a human being? How do we determine which action are performed rightly or wrongly? How do we arrive at a decision that a certain action is right or wrong? What criterion or standard do we employ in making such a decision or making such a judgment? What actually do we refer to when we say that a certain action is morally right or wrong? What sense does it make to say that "there is nothing good or bad but thinking makes it so"? Are there fundamental principles of morality? Is there a way of knowing them?[24] These questions face us in our everyday life, more especially in our interactions with others, since human being by nature is a social and communicating being.

Hence, the issue of ethics come into play whenever a public speaker faces an audience. Often a question arises, "does the mere ability to persuade entitle a man to the uninhibited use of the power that persuasion gives? This question, which is a fundamental one, appears as early as Plato's attack on the school of Sophists, in Athens, who were concerned with persuasion purely as a technique without reference to the ends to which it might be applied."[25] In an ideal world, as the Greek philosopher Plato noted, all public speakers would be truthful and devoted to the good of society. Yet history tells us that the power of speech is often abused – sometimes with disastrous consequences. Adolf Hitler was unquestionably a persuasive speaker. His oratory galvanized the German people into following one ideal and one leader. But his aims were horrifying and his tactics despicable. He remains to this day the ultimate example of why the power of the spoken word needs to be guided by a strong sense of ethical integrity.[26] This means that being an orator doesn't imply speaking without restriction or caution rather; you are bound to make your speeches ethical.

Ethical communication then is fundamental to responsible thinking, decision making, and development of relationships and communities within and across the context cultures, channels; and medial. Moreover, ethical communication enhances human worth and dignity by fostering truthfulness, fairness, responsibility, personal Integrity, and respect for self and others.[27] Knowing what ethical communication is all about will always open the eyes of every rightful thinking person to see the need why ethical communication is an imperative in all the processes of communication

PRINCIPLES FOR ETHICAL COMMUNICATION
In order to respect the dignity of man as a being endowed with reason and capable of communicating with each other, it is good to formulate an effective principle that will guide this prestigious ability (communication) from abuses and excess. Communication is not an individual enterprise which a person uses as freely as he wishes; rather it is a community enterprise – a sign of being-in-the-community. This means

that community sentiments must everywhere be respected in all matters of communication.

Hence, even though the principles of communication might not be able to solve all ethical difficulties pertaining to communication, yet it will go a long way in helping out and proffering solutions. "When communication loses its ethical underpinning and eludes society's control, it ends up no longer taking into account the centrality and inviolable dignity of the human person."[28] A good ethical principle will be the one that can make a sufficient scrutiny of actions before they are carried out. The major principles of ethical communication are discussed below:

Ethically Sound Intention:
It is not enough to make a good speech that is appealing to the ear, the intention of the speech also matters a lot. Oratory is not a painting exercise where the outer part of a vessel is well painted and presented without revealing the inner part. Neither is oratory a gamble where gaining personal advantage comes before other's good. These wrong approaches to communication are very unethical.

Hitler with his oratory led the Germans to war, invasion and genocide which have no ethical ground. This is also what some politicians, preachers, and crusade leaders do in various capacities. People use communication (most times through the media), "to block community and injure the integral good of persons: by alienating people or marginalizing and isolating them; drawing them into perverse communities organized around false, destructive values; fostering hostility and conflict, demonizing others and creating a mentality of "us" against "them"; presenting what is base and degrading in a glamorous light, while ignoring or belittling what uplifts and ennobles; spreading misinformation and disinformation, fostering trivialization and banality. Stereotyping – based on race and ethnicity, sex and age and other factors; including religion – is distressingly common in media."[29] These things are not worthy of any intention for communication.

Any form of communication that presents a wrong intention should not be accepted. The criterion for assessing a speech should not be sweetness of the presentation, rather the ethical soundness of its goal. Therefore, speakers should know that their speeches are being assessed always by well minded people and therefore should carry out proper ethical assessment of them before presenting them officially to the public.

A Well Prepared Speech:
It is unethical to embarrass people who left their various activities of life to come and listen to you. The business of oratory is not a type that can be meddled with – where every man sees as it pleases him without considering the sentiments of other. You are ethically bound to deliver a rich and well prepared speech.

The obligation of preparing a speech is double, analogous to the two wheels of a truck where one cannot work properly without the other. You have an obligation to yourself and an obligation to your audience both of which are inalienable. "The obligation to yourself, Luca said is obvious: the better you prepare, the better your speech will be. But the obligation to your listener is no less important. Think of it this way: the person who makes a bad 30-minute speech to an audience of 200 people wastes only a half hour of her or his own time. But that same speaker wastes 100 hours of the audience's time – more than four full days."[30] Think of such a speaker which Lucas has described as having wasted four full days, as liable to being sued. And imagine the grave legal consequences of such an act.

The preparation of speech will pass through a broad spectrum of analysing your speech ethically, the removal of every kind of error and misinformation in it, making your logic more grounded and backed up, knowing your topic many times greater than your audience and also making it as captivating as possible. This will help you to abide by one among other ethical principles.

Speech Guided with Sincerity:
Ethical speech should be guided by the sense of sincerity. It will be unethical for one to lie, confuse, deceive or practise any kind of dishonesty in the matters of speech making. Every human being in the community is united with his fellow human beings as a result of the mutual trust they have for each other. Once this trust is betrayed, the idea of community will shrink away.

Consider a situation where a speaker whom you used to trust for the past 30years was discovered to be lying in the current speech he is presenting to you. Though you only caught him lie for once, but this is enough for you to question your former assumptions and trust, and you will hardly like to hear him speak again. Your audience are listening to you because they are confident enough that you can be trusted and that what you are saying are worth relying on.

Betrayal of trust can bring an unimaginable harm most of which might be too late to correct. There is no lie which is small, no matter how you consider it. For Lucas, "there are more subtle forms of dishonesty that are just as unethical. They include juggling statistics, quoting out of context, misrepresenting the sources of facts and figures, painting tentative findings as firm conclusions, portraying a few details as the whole story, citing unusual cases as typical examples, and substituting innuendo and half-truths for evidence and proof. All of these violate the speaker's duty to be accurate and fair in presenting information."[31] Hence I will add plagiarism as one of these forms of dishonesty.

Consequently, the speaker must therefore say the truth and only those truths he is convinced in his heart of their truthfulness. There is no "resemblance", or "maybe" about the truth for an ethical speech, it must either be the truth or not the truth.

Communication should be Proportionate:
Ethical communication is intended to promote the common good so that each and every member of the group will benefit from it, and also be able to achieve fulfilment, and human dignity promoted through it.

Any communication which is in favour of one group at the expense of the other without any just cause is unethical. Communication is not a special property of some group, neither is it an instrument of intimidation, marginalization, superiority, and the like. "So much communication now flows in one direction only – from developed nations to the developing and the poor – and this raises serious ethical questions. Have the rich nothing to learn from the poor? Are the powerful deaf to the voices of the weak?"[32] Communication should rather be an instrument for promoting peace, solidarity, fairness and to crown it all, it should be a means of achieving the common good. And only in achieving common good with a good intention can this particular principle be realized.

Justin C. Nzekwe

Communication should be carried Out with Prudence and Respect:

It is unethical to talk to your audience without respect, or to use abusive languages on your audience no matter your position or status or what you think about your audience's personality. This is because everybody has a name to protect and guides this name and personality jealously. Nobody wants to be insulted in anyway. This is because our identity, worth, esteem, and other inner forces in us are attached to our personality, once we lose our personality, our whole self-worth is gone and this can be difficult to restore.

People usually have the conception that our names affect our personality, and the nicknames given to us reflect what people think about us. Therefore, when you use nicknames on people such as: "nigger", "bitch", "mmuom", inyamiri", "osu" etc. depending on culture, they tend to make such people to see themselves as minorities, inferiors, the never-do-well, rejected, and people who do not have equal dignity with others and therefore deserve no respect from their fellow human beings.

In a democratic setting 'where the freedom of speech is a basic right of all, people tend to seize such opportunity as an avenue to use abusive words on others such as engaging in character assassination, blackmailing of opponents, castigating rivals and using all sorts of calumny against others in order to achieve their selfish ends. The constitutions of some countries attempt to prevent this anomaly as much as they could, since it is ethically wrong. Therefore you are obliged as a speaker to avoid similar misdemeanours.

The ethical obligation is the same regardless of whether you are black or white, Christian or Muslim, male or female, gay or straight, liberal or conservative. A pro-environmentalist office seeker who castigates everyone opposed to her ideas as an "enemy of wildlife" would be on a thin ice ethically as a politician who labelled all his adversaries 'tax-and-spend liberals" when he knew fully that the charge was untrue. No matter what your stand on particular issues, you have an ethical responsibility to avoid name-calling and other tactics that harm the free and open expression of ideas.[33]

Lack of prudence and respect in communication can aggravate problems, it can breed prejudice, hate, segregation, rebellion, civil right violation and other crimes depending on the group or persons involved. Therefore speakers should try as much as possible to sieve out of their speeches anything that violates this particular ethical principle. When you address people like gentlemen, they would learn to be gentle. But if you address them with violence, they would apply resistance.

In conclusion, the ethics of communication is not meant for the communicators alone, the audience also has their responsibilities which range from their comportment during speech delivery. With the air of right reasoning, more ethics of communication can be discovered. Hence, the goal of these principles is not to know them for knowing sake, rather they are meant to be applied in our speeches as orators and in communication as communicating beings.

CHAPTER THREE

HOW TO PREPARE A SPEECH

Any academic adventure without a method will usually find itself in error and inconsistencies. And so is a speech without a method. Every speech has a way it is prepared which gives the speech a sense of aesthetics and makes it attractive to any ear or mind that comprehends it.

A speech is a way of communicating with another person. It is therefore aimless unless when directed to the second person. However, speech is a natural endowment and is one of the characteristics of a healthy man. Man by nature is the only animal that is capable of speaking or communicating through speech. Since man is lucky enough to be a speaking being, it is good also to learn how to organize man's speech into reasonable units of communication, since unorganized sets of speech are mere babblings without meaning. Hence Umunnakwe opines, "Speech writing and public speaking (speech delivery) are basically means of human communication by which our thoughts and feelings are expressed on contemporary issues. They are also means of sharing meaning with others. They are acts of creativity whose aesthetic power and effectiveness depend on the creative abilities of the speech writer or speaker."[34]

Furthermore, speech making is not just about making your voice heard, or initiating understanding, but also the effectiveness of the speech matters most. Some speeches are more effective than others, and the effectiveness of a speech is highly determined by the person who delivers the speech. If the speaker is able to communicate well with his/her audience, then the speech will be effective, but in a situation where he/she cannot communicate well, the speech will be absolutely ineffective. "Thus, simplicity, familiarity, and clarity of language, naturalness, concreteness and originality of speech and the dynamism and articulateness of the speaker are the hallmark of an effective speech writing and public speaking exercise."[35] Good speakers adopt every relevant means in order to achieve effectiveness in speech.

ELEMENTS OF SPEECH

Speeches are basically made up of three elements which characterize them. These elements are unavoidable in every speech presentation. They are: the speaker, audience and message.

Speaker:
The speaker is an unavoidable element of a speech; without the speaker, there will be no speech. In every speech somebody must be responsible; there is no possibility of an anonymous speech. In extreme cases where the speech writer must be unavoidably absent in a speech delivery, another person must stand on his behalf to deliver the speech. That is to say that "the substitute reader of another's speech and the ghost writer are the exceptions, not the rule, and do not violate the general truth that the speaker is an essential part of the speech."[36] Therefore the speaker plays a major role in speech.

Audience:
The audience can never be avoided in any speech delivery. They are the sole motivator of a speech, and without the audience, there will be no speech presentation. Thus since communication must involve the second person, and that

second person is the audience whose position can never be vacant, this audience can range from one person to any limitless number. In the case of mass audience, effective communication is better achieved with the help of the modern means of communication.

Message:
In very speech venue where the audience and speaker are both present there must be a message. This message is the goal of every speech, it is that which is communicated that gives meaning to speech. Once the message is initiated, communication has started. Without message, there will be no idea of speech presentation.

KINDS OF SPEECH
As individual members of a community, we often see ourselves deliver speeches in different capacities. It might be among friends, family members, church groups or other social gathering. A speech can either be formal or informal. This is mostly determined by some socio-linguistic variables or some guiding principles of speech presentation.

- The interlocutors involved in the speech
- The context/situation
- The purpose/objective
- The medium of communication
- The time
- The topic

Consequently, not only that a speech is either formal or informal, a speech can also be prepared or impromptu. Prepared speeches are planned ahead of time, it's usually written down and delivered on an official date, while an impromptu speech is unplanned speech, without prior information to the one who is to present the speech before the official date or moment. Impromptu speech depends on the speaker's experience, intelligence or the versatility of the speaker for its effectiveness. In addition, "a speech may also be said to be "extemporaneous" when a prepared speech is delivered speech is delivered without notes or delivered with a few brief notes instead of the full text of the prepared speech. It involves delivering a planned speech in the language of the moment."[37] Hence whatever type a speech might be, 'the onus of public speech is to transmit comprehension on the audience."[38]

However, there are certain situations that can necessitate a speech presentation, major among them are:

- Keynote address.
- Inaugural speech
- Valedictory speech
- Welcome speech
- Acceptance speech
- Anniversary speech
- Funeral Oration

Furthermore, there are many forms that these speech situations can take; it can either be in an Argumentative form, Descriptive form, or Expository form. These forms help to give shape to the speech, and save the speaker from a confused presentation of points.

Descriptive Form:
The word "description" means "illustrative detail". It tries to capture or describe a person, place, events, objects, animals, impression, and feelings or moods in such an imagery or vivid words that the listener can easily visualize or paint a clear mental picture of what is being talked about. The primary purpose of description is to portray sense impression and to indicate a mood. It tries to make the impression or

mood as vivid, real, or life-like for the reader as it was for the writer when he received the impression or observed the mood.[39] Description tries to stir the attention of the audience.

Care should be taken in the choice of words when describing, words that are precise and directly stress the points are adopted than general words. It takes a good speaker a lot of time to detail accordingly the precise meaning of general words like wonderful, interesting, good etc. Often, it is helpful to use one or more plans or systems of description. One typical plan is to move in a specific direction, example: from head to toe when describing a person, or perhaps clockwise when describing a room or place. The exact direction or order does not matter as long as you are consistent.

Another system of description is to use the five senses; still another, is to use the five W's of journalism by answering the questions "who, what, where, when and why or how?" when you describe a subject that moves – a person or moving object – it is wise to describe not only its appearance when standing still, but also its movement. In fact, whenever you write a description paper, it is wise to include as much action as possible: to make your audience see a movie whenever possible, and not just a painting or drawing.[40] There are different types of description which include: Directory description, technical description and Sensory description.

<u>Directory description:</u> this is the type that helps one to describe for the audience a particular person, places, points or things, Example: the man wearing a white short, a black shirt and red cap is my friend.

<u>Technical description:</u> this type is objective and offers proof to the audience. It is usually used in science. Example: a spider has eight legs.

<u>Sensory description:</u> this type creates a sensory impression in the audience. It involves using the five major sense organs of the body in description. Example: the taste of an orange.

In addition, Good organization of descriptive speech matters a lot. When one is describing an important event in a very poor way, he invariably, makes the important event unimportant because of the way he is describing it. A descriptive paper is organized very simply. You can start with a very short paragraph introducing or defining the subject, or a longer one that offers a particularly striking first description or overall summary. Next, you can write the body in as many or as few paragraphs as you need to fully describe the subject. Organizing these paragraphs according to one or more plans or systems often is helpful. Finally, you can write a concluding paragraph either briefly or at length, depending on whether you want to achieve an abrupt end or to provide some kind strong final description that you have saved for the last.[41] No matter what pattern of descriptive speech you use, always retain the goal which the speech is to describe.

Argumentative Form:

Human beings have different ways of viewing things. In our contemporary world, though views have been reduced to relativity and subjectivity, but some views are so clear that every good reasoning person can accept and testify the objectivity of it. The bid to offer an objective and concretely backed up views is the birth of arguments "We try to convince others to agree with our facts, share our values, accept our argument and conclusions, and adopt our way of thinking."[42]

Argument is usually between two parties, those who oppose and those who propose. But in some cases, one can simply bring out an opinion, argue on both sides of it and then draws the conclusion with his personal opinion. No opinion is accepted on a platter of gold without doubt, any opinion that is not doubtable is not arguable; therefore your ability to back your opinion with concrete reasons gives you an upper hand in your speech. Hence no matter the nature of an argument, the writer must always remind himself of the fact that sound reasoning remains an imperative. Without sound reasoning, one may succeed in deceiving oneself. Misapplied rhetoric deceives others and may lead to the rejection of an argument or may incur blames if discovered.[43] More so, truth is the basic tool in an argument – it is the correspondence of reason with reality. If the opinion is true, a good speaker will always win such an argument. Always support your arguments with facts and clarified values in the order of importance, draw your conclusion and persuade your audience to accept that your conclusion is based on agreed facts and shared values.

Meanwhile, there are several patterns of writing an argumentative form of speech that saves our speech from oversimplification and boredom on the audience.

Firstly, a typical argumentative paper often has what is called a "thesis" structure. It starts with an introduction that offers an interesting opening – a quotation, perhaps, or an interesting story, a statement of the main argument, and sometimes a list of the several reason (often three, but not necessarily so) to be given in support of this argument. Then, step by step, the reasons are given with supporting details such as quotations, facts, figures, statistics, and/or people's experiences. If the paper is short, there may be just one paragraph per reason. In a longer argumentative paper, there may be several paragraphs or even several pages per reason. At the end a conclusion provides a restatement of the main arguments and there may be a final interesting quotation or other details.

In the second pattern as an alternative form, the introduction is much the same, and often starts with an interesting aporia and provides the two (or more) possible answers. It may or may not state which answer it will choose in the end. The body is formed by having a section discussing the first possible answer with reasons and details supporting it, the second possible answer and its reasons and supporting details, and a final choice with a concluding interesting quotation or story.[44]

Expository Form:
The word exposition can be traced to a French origin "expose", meaning "to expose", "to explain' or "to clarify". Expository speech tries to explain more clearly, to inform, or report on how to arrive at a certain view of others. The goal of exposition is usually to elicit better understanding. By studying the method of exposition, "we are simply studying some of the ways our minds naturally work. We are not following an arbitrary scheme; we are following the ways in which we ordinarily observe and reason about our world. We are doing systematically something that ordinary living, in its hit-or-miss, unsystematic fashion, forces on us, quite naturally, all the time."[45] These qualities are what distinguished this method or form from every other forms of speech. It does not make use of argument to convince you, or to appeal to your imagination, it rather set the truth bare for you to judge yourself.

There are certain modes that can be adopted in exposition for an effective explanation: classification, definition, illustration, comparison and contrast, cause and effect. More so, exposition presents a subject in detail, apart from criticism, argument or development; that is, the writer elucidates a subject by analyzing it. Such writing is designed to convey information or explain what is difficult to understand.[46] However, a writer of expository speech should know how to present good information or opinions of others without adding his own. He should write or speak distinctly and should be objective in his exposition of ideas. He also should help his audience to understand any complex process, event and occurrences that should be exposed in the speech.

Consequently, expository speech is organized chronologically, its points are expressed sequentially; it starts from the first step and continues orderly till the last step. This will make the speech more comprehensible for the audience so as to assimilate the speech without doubts. For there to be a proper sequential arrangement of points in expository speech, there is also the need to adopt some transitional words like immediately, afterwards, currently, lastly, eventually, first, finally, furthermore etc.

For there to be an effective writing of expository speech, there are strategies that can guide a writer in expository writing:

> ➢ Include a topic sentence in each paragraph. The topic sentence of the first paragraph should present the topic of the entire explanation.

> ➢ Use transitional words to emphasize the relationships that exist among the ideas. Such words as; first for example, therefore,

furthermore, finally are necessary to move from one sentence or paragraph to the next.

➢ Define all terms that may be unfamiliar to the reader.

➢ Write a concluding sentence to tie up your explanation neatly.

The last sentence should let the reader know that the explanation has come to an end. A concluding sentence may summarize what has been explained or may serve as a comment on the explanation.[47]

Apart from the three major forms which a speech situation can take, there are other forms which might also be useful. A speaker should know how to manage the forms so as to make the speech rich for the audience consumption. A speech that does not place the interest of the audience as the measure of all things runs the risk of being a failure.

THE PURPOSE OF A SPEECH
For a speech to be effective it must have a focus; a purpose is what is always behind a speaker's mind whenever he is writing or making a speech. It is what a speaker wants to achieve in a particular speech presentation. A purposeless speech is a useless speech. Among the purposes of speech are:

- ❖ To inform,
- ❖ To persuade,
- ❖ To actuate,
- ❖ To entertain,

❖ To accept,

❖ To present, etc.

Speech to Inform:
We find ourselves everyday delivering an informative speech, explaining and giving out new ideas to our audience whether in the church, school, symposium and other social gatherings. We try to preoccupy a speech with explication of novelties within a speech knowingly or unknowingly.

However, the distinguishing mark of the informative speech is its *limited objective.* The sole purpose of the speech is to clarify, explain, describe, define, report, or otherwise broaden the audience's knowledge about some concept term, process, relationship, or other subjects. The speaker's goal is simple to enable the audience to grasp and then retain the material.[48]

A good informative speech does not require long stories or the use of ambiguous terms. Among its motive is to instill understanding in the audience. So therefore, the speaker should try as much as possible to be precise and direct to the point; he should employ simplicity and good illustration in every aspect of the speech.

If your (the speaker's) voice is as loud as a trumpet and your story as sweet as honey, but you could not hold the attention of your audience, it is like a sweet melody played in a lonely wilderness with no listener. The speaker should know that the audience is his shop and so gaining their attention is like making good sales for the day. Hence apply some flowery languages and other techniques that are good for hearing.

Finally, audiences are to be informed and not confused. Avoid anything that will make your audience get more confused or things that will affect the good comprehension of your audience. Make out few points and clarify them within your time limit. Don't accumulate all information in one speech and confuse your audience, tomorrow is another day to continue.

Speech to Persuade:
In a free and sentimental society where the freedom of opinion reigns supreme, we often find ourselves persuade or being persuaded by politicians, ministers, business men, scientists, philosophers etc. Everybody wants to give reasons why his own idea must be accepted as the best.

Persuasive speech is a kind of speech that aims at moving the mind of an audience to a predetermined way by influencing their attitude, beliefs, and values. A speaker that persuades has a cause at heart which he is about to fight; his intention might be to further a cause of action which exists but might be dormant, or to initiate a new cause. "The goal is fundamentally to win approval or secure a favorable attitude toward some belief the audience already holds."[49]

A persuasive speaker brings out controversial information, explains it, takes position, convinces, and pulls his audience to his position. Most speeches we hear everyday are persuasive in nature. They attempt to manipulate our wills with the power of reasoning and sentiments.

Speech to Actuate:
This speech is also popular in different fields especially in the area of politics. It serves basically to make people act. Even though that actuative speech can partially be grouped under persuasive speech, there is still a difference. Here, the goal is to mobilize the audience; to impel them to action of some sort; to move them to begin, continue, or cease some behavior. This goal will normally require some preliminary attention to both information and persuasion, but the overall thrust of the speech

will be to move the audience to behave in some particular way. The desired behavior might be voting, giving money, making a purchase, joining a cause, signing a petition, instituting some program, accepting Christ, or any other specific action. It is this additional dimension of action that distinguishes the actuative speech from the persuasive speech.[50] Always try as a speaker to distinguish between these two speech purposes in order to ensure clarity.

Speech to Entertain:
This refers to a humorous, funny or comic speech. It is geared towards making the audience happy – its purposes are amusement, laughter, and comedy. According to John-Ken, "the aim of this type of presentation is mostly to make the audience feel happy, but there may be hidden goals. For example: to reveal important truths or move ideas forward."[51]

Usually, entertaining speech intermingles with other purposes of speech: to inform, persuade, actuate, etc. in order to make them livelier. Litfin buttresses this fact when he opines that when seen in a broader sense the purpose to "entertain" does not supplant the other major purposes which a speech may have; *it rather complements them.* Whether our goal is to inform, persuade, or actuate matters little. In each of these cases we can and should attempt to make our speech broadly entertaining to our audience so that they are captivated by it.[52]

It must be pointed out that, a full entertaining speech sometimes is so fun-filled that it ends up making its ideas hidden from the audience. They end up making the audience feel that everything including the serious things the speaker communicated is meant to entertain them. However, only a gifted humorist can apply an effective humor. Effective humors are natural and spontaneous.

Speech to Present:
In a formal gathering where award, gifts or other forms of public recognition are to be presented, these are not presented without few words that explain to the audience why the gifts are presented and how the recipient merited the award. This form of speech is what is called "a presentation speech".

Presentation speech is always articulate and brief. Its major role is just to announce and to let the audience know the "why" of the occasion. In a presentation speech, the achievements of the recipient are open to the audience; they are made to know how the recipient merited the gifts, awards, or any other recognition.

Further, depending on the audience and the occasion, you may also need to discuss two other matters in a speech of presentation. First, if the audience is not familiar with the award and why it is being given, you should explain briefly – or at least allude to – the purpose of the award. Second, if the award was won in a public competition and the audience knows who the losers are, you might take a moment to praise the losers as well. Remember, sensitivity and good appropriation of values matter here.

Speech to Accept:
Ingratitude they say is a sign of incivility. We are usually grateful whenever we are rewarded in whatever capacity for our efforts or jobs. In the bid to show gratitude, we find ourselves delivering a speech most of which are usually impromptu.

In an acceptance speech, if is encouraged that you first of all thank your award presenters in a special way, for the initiative of the reward for excellence. Thanks also should be extended to all those who helped you to achieve such recognition whether by kind or cash. Make sure still to show the audience or fans that you are also grateful for their presence.

More so, every acceptance speech should portray a sign of humility, gratitude, happiness, and brevity if it must be attractive. An example of an acceptance speech is that delivered by Nelson Mandela while accepting the Congressional Gold Medal Award.[53]

KNOWING AN IDEA WORTH WRITING ABOUT

The central thing in developing a speech is having an idea of what you are about to write or speak. Any speech without an idea can well be referred to as useless. An idea is the central point that revolves round every speech. The Shorter Oxford Advanced Learners Dictionary defines idea as "the conception of a standard or principle to be realized or aimed at; the plan or design according to which something is created or constructed."[54] An idea in speech context also could be seen as something in a crude state, yet to be developed of which when developed will form a big thesis or speech.

In every speech, the speaker should always bear in mind that he is addressing or writing for his audience who are critical listeners. Nobody wants to be deceived and therefore everybody gives a critical ear in order to absolve the idea of a speech, criticize it and then know whether to accept it or not. Gage was of a similar view when he advised speech writers with these words, "As a writer, of course, you must expect your reader to ask the same question when you make assertion. You can't answer every 'why?' question that might be asked, but you can at least keep in mind that your word for anything you say matters."[55] Since our audience will always turn to be critical readers and listeners, we ourselves as speakers should also turn to be critical speakers.

However, every idea must be sentenced to the tribunal of critical reasoning, before it can qualify to be an idea. It must be able to stand the test of time. It must be able to withstand extreme criticism. It must be able to give a tough time to all question marks. And as Gage will say, "an idea is worth writing about when there's something of genuine interest in it for you and for those whom you wish to reach with it."[56] It is only such an idea which has passed through all these crucibles that is worth writing or discussing about.

CHOOSING A TOPIC

Among the basic problems many orators encounter when preparing to write a speech is the problem of choosing a topic. Some people are convinced of the need to prepare a speech, but have no idea of what to write on. They spend much of their time trying to imagine what to write on and still end up getting nothing. Except in some cases where people are assigned a topic to deliver, there are methods an orator can adopt in order to arrive speedily at an interesting and captivating topic. They are as follows:

Brainstorming:
Brainstorming is a method of generating ideas for speech topics by free association of words and ideas.[57] It is a way to get started with speech writing. After brainstorming, jot whatever comes to your mind about your subject either as a set of words or as informal phrases and you will be on the halfway to solving the difficulties of selecting a topic.

Montaigne was a Sixteenth century statesman, writer, and philosopher who retired from public life at the age of 38. He retired so that he could put his psychic house in order, while he writes books. He later went into brainstorming and with reference to the ideas that crashes around his head he says, "…like a runaway horse, (my mind) gives itself a hundred times more trouble than it took for others, and gives birth to so many chimeras and monsters, one after another, without order or purpose, that in order to contemplate their ineptitude and strangeness at my pleasure. I have begun to put them in writing, hoping in time to make my mind ashamed of itself."

All Montaigne wants to explain is that those disorderly products of brainstorming need to be orderly arranged by an experienced mind in order to make them understandable and useful.

For you to make an effective brainstorming you will need to time yourself; for instance by giving yourself about ten to twenty minutes to do a serious work of the mind, you will develop a sense of seriousness, consciousness and also a time to get relieved from mind labor.

You are advised also to avoid the job of analysis which is not the task of brainstorming but rather a post-brainstorming job. It creates more labor for your brain, and makes your brain processing slow. When brainstorming, try and be smart in order to jot down immediately whatever knowledge or information that comes to your mind no matter what kind of information they are, whether relevant or irrelevant, reasonable or unreasonable, organized or unorganized. However, the list of words you have jotted forms the source from where one can get the theme or topic of a speech.

Association of Ideas:
If the formal method (brainstorming) doesn't work out well for you in getting a good topic, try the method of association of ideas. This method is a method that works with the senses either through the internal or external senses. But more often, it works with the internal senses (common sense, fantasy,

memory and instinct) because the external senses are *ancillia* internal senses.

However to clarify the work of the senses in the association of ideas we talk about the speculative power of fantasy which is capable of going beyond our imagination in order to create an idea. Hence mondin argues that, with the *speculative* function, the fantasy can occur with the formation of the intellectual constructions of science, philosophy, and theology. In these fields, every project is prepared by the fantasy, especially in the moment of the formulation of hypotheses, and is subsequently assisted by the fantasy in its moment of their illustration. The great truths of theology, metaphysics, and physics, formulated with rigor by the intellect, become more accessible to out comprehension after the fantasy has succeeded in devising myths, symbols, and images to make these truths assume a concrete appearance before our eyes.[58]

More so, it might be ridiculous to say that we are not the determinant of the ideas we get through this means, we just leave our mind to wallow down the solitude of the world of ideas or within the confines of external world to pick information as much as it pleases. Thus the British empiricist idealist Bishop observed this too when he said, "as far as the power I have over my thoughts, I must note that the ideas perceived with the sense do not depend on my will. When in the full light of day I open my eyes, it is not in my power if I see or not, or to determine which particular objects present themselves to my sight; and thus as well for the hearing and the other senses, the ideas impressed on them are not the creatures of my will."[59] Though you are not the architect of those ideas in the proper sense, but you are going to be the one to systemize them.

Then this is the process to follow; get your writing materials around, draw tables or columns and then add keys to the tables. The keys are going to serve as a compass in your mental navigation towards exploring a new and good topic. Try not to forget your keys, you can always write it and keep it for anytime you want to select topics. The keys are: place, things, person, events, occupation, concepts, books processes, problems, plans and policies, natural occurrences. When you have finished listing the keys in the form of a heading, then write under each key anything that comes to your mind that is related to it.
For instance:

PLANS & POLICIES
Computer voting
Railway security
School feeding Immunization
Computer identity cards
Ballistic fingerprinting
Rights of children Electronic

PERSONS
Pope Frances
Nnamdi Kalu
Goodluck Jonathan
Nelson Mandela
Mohammed Ali
Martin Luther King, Jr.
Bill Gate
+Fulton John Sheen
Nzekwe Nonso
Barack Obama
Réne Descartes
Kofi Annan

However, when you are able to scan out from your mind all these issue and to categorize them under different keys to which they belong, then you have already reached the threshold of the answer to the relevant speech issues bordering you. The next step is a lesser job; read those things again and know whether anything will strike your brain as you are doing so. Example, when you come around the key "Person", and discover a name like "Martin Luther King, Jr.", it can help you to remember to deliver a speech concerning "Non-Violent Movement: A Solution to Corrupt Government Practices", or under "Plans and policies", the sight of the concept of "immunization" might help you to develop a theme like: "Why Immunization Is An Imperative For Children In Africa". Thus, association of ideas helps you to develop new ideas, to refresh old ideas and to construct interesting themes for speeches.

SOURCES OF SPEECH

There are lots of places one can gather helpful hints in preparing a speech; although in some cases, these ways may not be perfect. But the speaker can always develop the little information gathered by appealing to his common sense through a prudent generalization or association. Here are some of the major sources of gathering helpful information for a speech:

Magazines and Newspapers:
These contain more recent information; opinions and observations of what might form the topic or the content of your speech. This will give you insight into a wider view and determine your stand in your speech. A speech deduced from magazines and newspapers is usually more realistic, and relates more to the daily life of the people.

Television and Radio:
These are among the fastest means of communication. A speaker can gain information here and pass it to the audience in not more than three minutes the incident occurred. It enhances the attractiveness and appreciation of a speech because it is often realistic just like other information media and it also discusses us and our environment.

A speaker who resorts to the audio-visual media like radio and television is often seen as a versatile speaker. Therefore they are good sources of information hunting.

Internet:
This is the father of modern information technology. Uncountable barrels of information pass through the internet every second of the day. Through internet, you can get any information that can form your speech. You can gain the opportunity of chatting or interviewing people live through the internet to gain the information needed, you can also browse through ancient and modern documentations, articles, books, events happening even at that moment. You can also write and receive messages through it. It gives you access to visual and oral representation of all these information directly from your private system (computer).

The search for information in the internet is facilitated by various search engines like:
YAHOO: **www.yahoo.com**
MSN: www.msn.com
MYSEARCH: **www.mysearch.com**
GOOGLE: **www.google.com** etc.

However, be careful always to filter the information browsed in order to differentiate between junk and real information, since the internet is subject to error and misinformation.

Encyclopedia and Dictionaries:
These contain more of documentations, definitions or explication of terms, histories, etc. According to Nworgu, they are (Encyclopedia and Dictionaries) very *useful* for accurate definitions and for clearer understanding of the specialized meanings of key terms and concepts in the study.[60]

Explication of terms is very relevant in speech delivery. Speakers should as much as possible to avoid the use of ambiguous words or words that cannot communicate effectively to their audience. The major task of encyclopedia and dictionaries is to clear the ambiguity of words and make the speech and meanings simple and easy to grasp.

Books:
Books here refer mostly to text books. These enable speakers know opinions of authorities about the particular theme they are about to deal with. A speech can also be motivated mainly from the information gotten from a book read some time ago or some striking questions an author raises in a book. The use of books when preparing speeches serve to back them up with authoritative evidence, thus making them convincing.

Journals or Periodicals:
The inspiration of many academic speeches usually comes from academic works like journals or periodicals. They contain recent and in-depth research of tropical issues. In other words, "the knowledge contained in them represents the most recent in the field."[61] They break information to the barest minimum; some primary works of some authors are too ambiguous to be understood, but when another author analyses it in a journal, the clarity of the information in the

book becomes more effective. Effective use of journals or periodical makes a speech 'super'.

Observation:
This is an important way of getting information, which has always proved helpful to speakers during speech preparation and even up to the place of presentation. "Observation involves watching people, events, situations or phenomena and obtaining first hand information relating to particular aspects of such people events, situation or phenomena. Information relating to certain aspects of human behaviors can only be obtained in the particular setting where such behaviors are exhibited."[62] The purpose of observation is to make information a firsthand material without unnecessary predictions and suppositions.

However, caution must be taken by a speaker in the area of the objectiveness of an observation can either be participant or non-participant. In the former case, the observer is usually part of the people he is observing for a longer time and should have known various behaviors about the people he is observing after a long personal experience. The latter case refers to when the observer is not a member of the setting, but is opportune to observe the behavior of a strange set of people where he does not belong.

Documentaries/ Histories:
Tell me the historical records of past events and I will accurately predict future events. Historians are highly gifted in this particular source of information gathering. The speaker should search and see if there is any documentation on the people he/she is writing on, in the form of minutes of previous meeting, announcements, rules and regulations, charters, published books and so on. As a general advice,

never forget histories, it is always a torch light into the future.

Past Experience:
It is only a stupid man that forgets and doesn't from his experiences. Good speakers are mainly those that first of all consider the audiences sentiments by placing themselves in the shoes of their audience in order to know the theme to address them on, and the way to go about it. Use call information you have gained about your audience, but if you have no experience about your audience at all, then try to compare them with the knowledge you gained from a similar audience. Your experience in oratory will always lead you through every difficult situation pertaining to this revered profession.

Questionnaires:
This is a means of gaining information for a speech topic or even the body of a speech. A speaker is not omniscient and does not know everything; he therefore needs the help of others to gain relevant information for his speeches.

Questionnaires are distributed in the form of questions with answers options for the people to air their views by filling in their choice answers. The questionnaire could be used to obtain information on a number of issues. It could be used to obtain information on the distribution of a group of people in terms of gender, state, qualification, age, socio-economic, status, working experiences etc. It could also serve to provide information for assessing certain situations that can enable us to obtain data on the feelings and perceptions of a group of people towards certain things such as their attitudinal disposition towards the current issues and events. Though there are different types of questionnaire, but all of them gear towards gathering required information determined by the researcher. Hence, a good questionnaire should be: consistent, relevant, useable, clear quantifiable and legible.

Interview:
This is a great means of information gathering. Like questionnaire, an interview can be effective up to a few minutes before the speech presentation. A good interview gives you facts that will make your speech more realistic and concrete.

However, a lot of risk is faced by a person using interview as a means of gathering information, this is because, sometimes, the correspondence might not open up or might give false information. Also, a bad frame of questions might debar an interviewer from getting the right answer to his questions. Nworgu advised that "the question have to properly framed in such a way that the interviewee can easily understand what information is being asked for."[63] Hence, an interviewer should establish a rapport between him and the interviewee. He should avoid an extreme use of technical or ambiguous terms. He should talk and interview within a context for a concrete information. He should also learn to probe questions and avoid non-leading questions.

Furthermore, what makes an interview what it is, is the verbal interaction, recorded responses, and the flexibility associated with it. Thus, interview is a great and unavoidable means of gaining information for a speech.

Finally, the question of how to prepare a speech has no fixed rule that is not reviewable. There are so many ways of preparing a speech in order to make it accomplish its purpose without necessarily violating the ethics of communication. This chapter has gone a long way in providing us with the major ways and means of preparing an effective speech. Try as much as possible to have a purpose for your speech in order not to waste your time in useless adventures. Your focus will guide you through out your speech preparation.

HOW YOUR IDEA CAN LEAD YOUR AUDIENCE
A speaker is like an armor bearer to his audience, he leads the way which his audience follows. Tibbette sees him as a professional guide in a jungle who leads his group of travellers towards an objective by avoiding wild animals, pitfalls, and quicksand traps.[64] The high position a speaker is placed should not be messed up. A speaker should rather try to follow a methodology which will enable him to communicate in a way that his audience will follow his line of thought. No matter how good an intention of a speaker is in communicating, if the ideas communicated are not clear to his audience, the entire effort is wasted. In every speech, try to make your idea clear when you:

Begin with a Familiar Idea:
Your speech should not be too abstract or complex at the beginning. You should always try to arrange your idea in an acceleration order – from inertia to a uniform acceleration. Don't just begin a speech with unfamiliar idea, lest from that time you lose the attention of the audience till the end of your speech. You might begin with a joke, information that they know of, and from there, you move to the more complex ideas.

Have a Sequential Arrangement of Ideas:
Try to write your speech in a way that the actions and events are arranged in an orderly way. There is no way you can begin to write on what happened in 2006, while you are yet to write what happened year back. Arrange your ideas in a pyramid shape, so that after the base, comes several other steps before the peak.

However, try also to arrange the information in the order of importance: the least important comes first, while the most important comes last. Carefully, "you build up interest if you leave your best point until last. If you give readers your best idea first, they may quit reading in the middle of your paper."[65]

Furthermore, in this method, there can be few exceptions where the most important comes first. But in any case, the type of audience has an important role to play in the choice of an arrangement of ideas.

Use a Directional:
There are some words that can lead an audience to the threshold of meaning. They are transitory in nature and as Tibbetts will always say, *"Use Single Word or Phrase Transitions.* Transitions point forward and backwards. They are the reader's signposts; without them he or she might easily get lost."[66] Hence, transitions are divided into those that count in order and those that can lead an audience by the hand and smoothen their ways.

Here are some typical transitional words and phrases:[67]

- ✓ To explain or introduce ideas: *for instance, for example. Such as, specifically, in particular, to illustrate, thus*
- ✓ To count or separate *ideas: second, third (but no/firstly, secondly, thirdly), moreover, in addition, another, furthermore, also again, finally.*
- ✓ To compare idea: *likewise, similarly, in the some way.*
- ✓ To contrast or qualify ideas: however, *or the other hand on the contrary, but.*
- ✓ To show cause or effect: *as a result, consequently, therefore, thus.*

Use Emphasis/Repetition:
Although it is advised to apply variety in the use of words, professional speakers apply a lot of repetition in the use of important words that embody a major idea, so as to help retain the word in the audience's memory. You can apply emphasis also when you have talked for a longer time and you now want to draw your audience back to an important idea you have related before, you can re-emphasis the words or sentence. More still, Tibbetts encourages speakers to use repetition creatively; you may repeat certain words or phrases in order to keep the reader's mind firmly on the subject. Sometimes you can change the grammatical form slightly in order to prevent the repetition from becoming a bore.[68]

GIVE YOUR SPEECH A STAND OR CONCLUSION
A lot of speakers find themselves preparing a wonderful speech from the introduction to the body of the speech only to end the speech without a conclusion or any stand.

Words like *therefore, so, because* and the likes have a very significant role to play in a speech. It gives the speech a stand or helps in drawing the conclusion of the speech. Every speech is made up of both premise and conclusion. This premise and conclusion can appear in many places within a speech depending on the idea that is being communicated. But bear in mind that any premise(s) that is set up in a speech must have a conclusion attached to it especially when such a speech is argumentative in nature. So, avoid giving neutral speeches or raising unjustifiable opinions. If you have ever thought of putting up a matter or a point to address, you are also bound to justify your point by drawing a conclusion.

CHAPTER FOUR

HOW TO USE A DILEMMA

Dilemma as a rhetorical instrument dates back to the ancient Greeks, who are more interested in rhetorical speech making not minding the logical coherency. Rhetorically, dilemma is perhaps the most powerful instrument of persuasion ever devised. It is a devastating weapon in controversy. Dilemma helps to make a head way out of a difficult situation since dilemma has a little logical importance.

Dilemma as the name suggests is the argument-form that helps a speaker to force an opponent or an audience into a rigid corner by presenting unpleasant alternatives from which a choice must be made verbally or non-verbally. When one has been subjected to such a situation, he is said to be impaled by the horns of dilemma. However, it is wrong, to assume that all dilemma offer unwelcome choices.

Dilemma may be defined rather formidably as an argument containing a compound, hypothetical major premise and a disjunctive minor premise, which affirms alternatively the antecedent(s) of the major.[69] The conclusion whether of denying or affirming is either categorical or disjunctive. When the argument is more than two, it is said to be a *trilemma, tetralemma* etc.

KINDS OF DILEMMA:
Dilemma is majorly divided into four: simple constructive, Simple destructive, complex constructive and complex destructive. The dilemma is said to be constructive when the

consequents are denied. The dilemma is also said to be simple when there is only one antecedent and complex when there are two antecedents.[70]

SIMPLE CONSTRUCTIVE DILEMMA:
If I pray I shall go to heaven;
And if I sing I shall go to heaven;
Either I pray or I sing; I shall go to heaven.

        OR

If I pray or sing, I shall go to heaven;
Either I pray or I sing;
I shall go to heaven.

COMPLEX CONSTRUCTIVE DILEMMA:
An example of dilemma is what happened during the American civil war. James Mason and John Slidell were Confederate Commissioners to Britain and France. On learning that they had left Havana for England on the British Ship *Trent*, Union Captain Wilkes' stopped the *Trent*, and removed them. Wilkes' action was contrary to international law. The British Government demanded that the U.S. release the prisoners and apologize for Wilkes' action. 'Lincoln and Seward were in a dilemma. If they did not satisfy Britain they might find themselves with another war on their hands. If they did, public opinion- which had made a hero of Wilkes – would be outraged.'

> If we satisfy Britain, then the United States public will be outraged. If we do not satisfy Britain, then there might be war. Either we satisfy Britain by releasing the Prisoners and apologizing for Wilkes' action, or we do not satisfy Britain. Therefore, either the United States public will be outraged or there will be war.[71]

COMPLEX DESTRUCTIVE DILEMMA:

If Congress is not in a state of anarchy, then it does not have leadership.

If Congress does not block the president, then it does not have leadership.

Either Congress has leadership or it does not have leadership.

Therefore either Congress is in a state of anarchy or it is blocking the president.

SIMPLE DESTRUCTIVE DILEMMA

If a body moves, it must either move in the place where it is, or in the place where it is not.

But it can neither move in the place where it is, nor in the place where it is not.

Therefore, it cannot move.

CONFRONTING THE DILEMMA:
The ability to confront a dilemma helps you to easily escape the often preceding unpleasant conclusion. In order to do this, one does not need to search for a fallacy in the argument, for the dilemma as such is not invalid. "The dilemma is a rhetorical scheme. Thus to confront it one has to be rhetorical too; one has to demonstrate that the propositions constituting the dilemma have 'material faults.'"[72]

There are three ways of confronting a dilemma: taking it by the horns, escaping between the horns, and rebuttal.

TAKING IT BY THE HORNS:

This means accepting one or both of the antecedents ("horns") and then denying that either one or both of the consequents follow Example;

If I read I shall be intelligent, and if I write,

I shall be intelligent; either I read or I write;
Therefore I shall be intelligent.

The dilemma can be taken by the horns by denying a part or all of the major premise, which is a conditional: one can argue that writing will make one tired and therefore become ignorant.

If I read, I shall be misinformed,

And if I write I shall be tired and be ignorant;

either I write or I read; therefore I will be ignorant.

ESCAPING BETWEEN THE HORNS:

This is possible when the disjunction in the minor premise is not completely exhaustive of all alternatives.

EXAMPLE:

"If I vote for the Republicans, I shall be voting against Labor, and if I vote for the Democrats, I shall be voting for Inflation. But I shall vote either Republican or Democrats, I shall be voting for Inflation. But I shall vote either Republican or Democratic, therefore I shall vote either against Labor or for Inflation."

Here it may be readily pointed out that I could vote for some other party than the Republican or Democratic, and hence would not be impaled on the "horns" (alternatives) of the dilemma, for I have escaped them by discovering another alternative on the other hand. So, in a case where the minor premise presents us with a strong disjunction an escape between the horns is precluded. Thus:

"If we have war, then there will be Inflation; and if we have peace, we shall maintain a sound economy. We shall have either war or peace; therefore we shall either have inflation or maintain a sound economy."

Here it would be virtually impossible to discover any other alternative to war or peace.

REBUTTAL:
A rebuttal is a counter-dilemma with a conclusion that is opposed to the original conclusion. It is effective because it reconstructs what appears to be almost the same dilemma and arrives at an opposite conclusion.

The rebuttal is accomplished by (1) negating each consequent in the major premise and (2) transposing the consequents in the major premise.[73] Any counter-dilemma may be used in rebuttal, but ideally it should be built up out of the same ingredients (categorical propositions) that the original dilemma contained.[74]

EXAMPLE OF REBUTTAL:

Example 1:
A classical example of rebuttal concerns the following argument of an Athenian mother attempting to persuade her son not to enter politics:

The Art of Oratory

If you say what is just, men will hate you; and if you say what is unjust, the gods will hate you; but you must either say the one or the other; therefore you will be hated

Her son rebutted the dilemma with the following dilemma:

If I say what is just, the gods will love me; and if I say what is unjust, men will love me. I must say either the one or the other therefore I shall be loved.

Example 2:

This sort of rebuttal does not refute, but only directs attention to a different aspect of the same situation. An example is this dilemma, advanced by an "optimist"

If I work, I earn money; and if I am idle, I enjoy myself. Either I work or I am idle. Therefore either I earn money or I enjoy myself.

A "pessimist" might offer the following counter dilemma:

If I work, I don't enjoy myself; and if I am idle, I don't earn money.
Either I work or I am idle. Therefore either I don't earn money or I don't enjoy myself.

Example 3:

This dilemma occurred in the celebrated lawsuit between Protagoras and Euathlus. Protagoras was a teacher who lived in Greece during the fifth century B.C. He taught many subjects but specialized in the art of pleading before juries. Euathlus wanted to become a lawyer, but, not being able to pay the required tuition, he made an arrangement according to which Protagoras would teach him but will not receive payment until Euathlus wins his first case. When Euathlus finished his course of study he delayed going into practice. Tired of waiting for his money, Protagoras brought a suit against his former pupil for the tuition money that was owed.

Unmindful of the adage that the lawyer who tries his own case has a fool for a client, Euathlus decided to plead his own case in court. When the trial began, Protagoras presented his side of the case in a crushing dilemma:

> If Euathlus loses this case, then he must pay me (by the judgment of the court); if he wins this case, then he must pay me (by the terms of the contract). He must either: lose or win this case. Therefore Euathlus must pay me.

The situation looked bad for Euathlus, but he had learned well the art of rhetoric. He offered the court the following counter-dilemma in rebuttal.

> If I win this case, I shall not have to pay Protagoras (by the judgement of the court); if I lose this case, I shall not have to pay Protagoras (by terms of the contract, for then I shall not have won my first case). I must either win or lose this case. Therefore I do not have to pay Protagoras.
> If you were the judge, what will be your verdict?

Furthermore, dilemma is one of the best *organum* for refuting argument. Proper knowledge of dilemma saves you form dumb-foundness when challenged with arguments. It gives you an easier way to always escape any clutches arguments might pose. Cicero advises that in any challenging argument your opponents' proof must be countered, either by contradicting the arguments chosen to establish it, or by showing that their desired conclusion is not supported by their premises; or, if you do not so rebut it, you must adduce on the opposite side some proof of greater or equal cogency.[75] This can only be achieved by a firm knowledge of the dilemma as a strategy of rhetorics.

The Art of Oratory

CHAPTER FIVE

MASTERING SPEECH SOUNDS AND TECHNIQUES

It is always good and safer to learn an art from the scratch. Mastering speech sounds and other aspect of speech, equip us better for the more technical aspect of speech delivery. When we do not know how to pronounce words properly, or unable to use the right choice of words in our various sentences, we end up communicating distractions instead of the good message we intend to pass across. Speakers with poor knowledge of grammar are also poor public speakers unless they are comedians.

SPEECH SOUNDS
Speech is a form of communication which is vocalized. It is produced through the syntactic combination of lexicals and names that are formed from very large sets of vocabularies. Every normal human being is endowed from birth with the capacity for speech which can be developed further. Speech when perfected can be used as a means of exchanging information, expressing feelings and even for entertainment. Speech and its corollary listening, work together. The presence of Speech creates the necessity for listening, in order to understand the sound.

Characteristic of Speech
    a. It is a human quality: Human being is the only living organism that is capable of producing what qualifies for a speech. Even though the animals make various

familiar sounds, these sounds do not qualify for a speech.

b. It is vocalic: Speech is verbal. It is a sound produced in and through the vocal organs – the trachea, nose and mouth cavity. Any other sounds which do not pass through these medium do not qualify for a speech.

c. It is articulated: Speech is not just all about producing sound, it is rather the production of organize sound. In the speech process, there is the interplay of vocal organs in organized manner, depending of the sound the speaker intends to produce. However, any unorganized and incomprehensible sound produced through the vocal tract does not qualify for a speech.

PHONETICS AND PHONOLOGY

Phonetics is the study of human speech sounds and how they are produced and how they are perceived. While Phonology on the other hand, is the study of the speech sound of any language. It is concerned with the abstract, grammatical characterization of systems of sounds or signs. Phonetics is usually a delicate part of every language especially for non-native speakers. Most non-native speakers usually master how to write the language before learning how to speak it, and are therefore faced with the challenge of how to pronounce words properly. They are often left at the mercy of the teacher who guides them through the pronunciations of alphabets and words. They are sometimes faced with the challenges of discovering the sharp variances in pronunciations between two speakers as a result of changes over time, environment, health challenges, and other minute factors. They also discover that no matter the effort one put in while learning the phonetics, the native tongue still have a great influence of the persons pronunciations. They also discover that "there are even variations in sounds coming from one speaker from time to time depending on moods and circumstances. Many of us who have had cause to record, our voices on cassettes from time to time would realize this when we play back such cassettes. We continue to make efforts towards standardizing our phonetics."[76] These challenges do not deter us from learning English phonetics, rather it guides us to learn it better by making effort to overcome all those challenges and to learn the right phonetics.

However, Phonetics can be mastered through, living among native speakers, teachers of the language, listening to special programs by native speakers, listening to BBC, CNN, etc., listening to a good language aid, sharing the culture of native speakers, developing interest in it and practicing always.

VOWEL
Etymologically, the word vowel comes from a Latin word *vocalis* which means "vocal" (that is something which has connection with voice). However, in English usage, "vowel" often refers to both vowel sounds and symbols used in identifying them in writing. A vowel in phonetics therefore can be defined as a frictionless sound pronounced with an open vocal tract. While pronouncing a vowel, the tongue does not touch the mouth cavity, teeth and lips. Phonologically, a vowel is the sound that forms the nucleus of a syllable.

A vowel is made up of twelve monophthong (iː, ɪ, e, æ, ʌ, ɑː, ɒ, ɔː, u, uː, ɜː, ə) and eight diphthongs (eɪ, aɪ, ɔː, aʊ, əʊ, ɪə, ɛə, ʊə), making it a total of twenty sounds. There are two types of vowel sounds, the monophthong and the diphthong. The monophthong or the pure vowels as often referred, are usually single, and produced as a sound with the tongue and other organs remaining stationary. Diphthong is made up of two paired vowels. Unlike in pure vowels, in diphthong, the tongue glides from one point to another in order to produce the sound.

Fig. 5. 1: Below is a conventional vowel chart

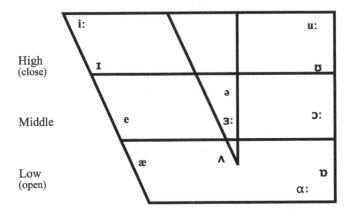

CONSONANTS

Consonants are those speech sounds that are not vowels. They are articulated with complete or partial closure of the vocal tract; the air flow is interrupted or limited by the position of the tongue, teeth or lips. Consonants cannot be pronounced without a vowel. However, even though there are twenty-one (21) consonant **letters** in English, there are actually twenty-four (24) unique consonant **sounds** in English speech (**b, d, g, v, ð, z, ʒ, dʒ, l, r, w, j, m, n, ŋ, p, t, k, f, θ, s, ʃ, h, tʃ**). Consonants usually appear in two groups: the pure consonants and affricates. The chart below helps us to understand the manner, and the place of production of the sounds of consonants.

Fig. 5.2: Consonant Chart.

Manner of Production	Voiceless	Voiced	Place of Production
Plosive	P t k	B d g	Bilabial alveolar velar
Fricative	F θ s ʃ h	V ð z ʒ 	Labiodental dental alveolar palato-alveolar glottal
Affricate	tʃ	dʒ	Palatal
Lateral		L	Alveolar
Approximant		R w j	Alveolar bilabial palatal
Nasal		M n ŋ	Bilabial alveolar velar

Places of Articulation for the Consonants:

a. **Bilabials:** These are sounds produced with the two lips – the upper and lower lips: [**p, b, m, w**]. Examples in words: pen, cab, name, wait.
b. **Labiodentals:** These sounds are produced with the upper teeth and the inner lower lips: [**f,v**]. Examples in words: few, void.
c. **Dentals:** The sound here is produced with the tip of the tongue on or near the inner surface of the upper teeth: [**θ,ð**]. Examples in words: thin, their.

d. **Alveolars:** These sounds are produced through the front part of the tongue placed near the tooth ridge [t, d, s, z, n, l]. Examples in words: tour, door, say, zoom, never, lamb.
e. **Palatals:** These sounds are produced with the tongue blade or body near the hard palate: [tʃ, dʒ, s, ʒ, r]. Examples in words: chain, judge, shy, measure, red.
f. **Velars:** These sounds are produced with the tongue body on or very close to the soft palate: [k, g, ŋ]. Examples in words: keg, go, sing.
g. **Glottal:** The sound here is produced by the passing of air through the windpipe and through the vocal cords: [h]. Example in words: hot, hat.

ORGAN OF SPEECH

These are the components of the body that produce the sounds of language. Many organs contribute to the sounds of language, but we are going to occupy ourselves with the eight major parts of human speech organs: Lips, Teeth, Tongue, Uvula, Alveolar Ridge, Hard Palate, glottis and Velum (Soft Palate).

Lips: Human lips are vital in creating sounds. It can easily form different shapes and make relevant movements so as to produce varieties of sounds as when desired. The lips are useful in the performing of wind instruments, and makes whistling possible. The lips help to create the labial, bilabial sounds (eg. /p/, /b/, /m/, /hw/, /w/) and labio-dental consonant sounds (eg. /f/ and /v/).

Teeth: The teeth functions by shaping the lips. It also functions as a passive articulator by combining with the tongue, and through controlling the movement of the air in the mouth, so as not to escape the mouth. The teeth usually create the labio-dental sounds (e.g. /f/, /v/) and lingua-dental sounds (e.g. /ð/, /θ/).

Tongue: The tongue is a key and active instrument in the production of sounds. It makes varieties of movements around the mouth, takes different shapes, and in combination with many of the other organs in order to articulate a speech.

Uvula: By working together with the back of the throat, the palate, and air coming up from the lungs, it creates a number of guttural and other sounds. By stopping the air from moving through the nose, the uvula helps to make nasal consonants sounds.

Alveolar Ridge: This is the ridge behind the upper front teeth. It is located between the roof of the mouth and the upper teeth. In contact with the tongue, the alveolar ridge helps us in making different sounds known as alveolar sounds. To produce sounds like /s/, the air from the lungs passes continuously through the mouth, while the tongue is raised sufficiently close to the alveolar ridge to cause friction as it partially blocks the air that passes.

Hard Palate: This is the thin horizontal bony plate of the skull, located in the roof of the mouth. When articulating a speech, the tongue touches and taps the palates. This interaction between the tongue and the hard palate is essential in the formation of certain speech sounds like /t/, /d/, and /j/.

Glottis: This is the combination of the vocal folds and the space between the vocal folds. It is used in controlling the vibration made by the vocal chords, in order to make different sounds. The sound produced only by the glottis is known as glottal. Example is /h/ sound.

Velum (soft palate): The special sound produced when the tongue hits the velum is known as velar consonant. In order to produce the oral speech sound, the velum should have holes to separate the oral cavity from the nose. When the separation is not complete, it allows the air to escape through the nose during the speech process, thereby leading to an imperfect speech sound known as hyper nasal speech.

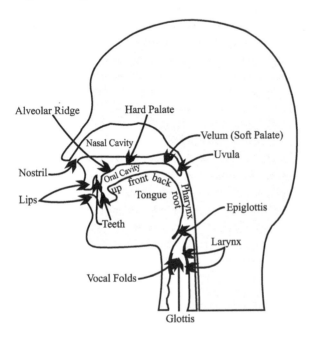

Fig. 5.3: Diagram of the vocal tract with the nasal and oral cavity.

PARTS OF SPEECH

In linguistic studies, words are considered to be the smallest units of a language which have distinctive meanings. There words have different classes. Parts of speech are therefore the classes into which words may be grouped with reference to their functions in a sentence. They are category of words with similar grammatical properties. However, to identify a part of speech a word belongs, one must first of all consider the use of the word in a sentence. A good knowledge of part of speech disposes us for a smooth communication and skillful writing. In this context, we are going to limit ourselves with the eight commonly known English parts of speech. These includes: noun, pronoun, verb, adjective, adverb, preposition, conjunction and interjection.

NOUN

This is the most common part of the speech. The word noun is etymologically derived from a Latin word, *"nomen"* which means "name". Nouns therefore are basically naming words. It is the name of a person, animal, place, thing, or idea.

Classification of nouns

Proper nouns: Proper noun usually starts with a capital letter. They are the names of persons, places, things, events, etc. Examples: Amaka, Nonso, Justin, Nigeria, Igbo, Mercedes Benz, Christmas, etc.

Common nouns: They are the generic names of persons or things. Examples: Man, tree, car, etc. However, Common noun can further be subdivided into: Abstract, Concrete, countable and uncountable nouns.
    Abstract nouns: Are those which we can't perceive through our five senses. They refer to the state, quality or action of persons or things. Examples: joy, goodness, bravery, gentleness, etc.
    Concrete nouns: They are those tangible things which can also be perceived through our five senses. Examples: spoon, plate, book, etc.

Countable nouns: These nouns take plural or singular forms, and make use of definite and indefinite articles. However, they can be counted. Examples: an office, offices, the offices.

Uncountable nouns: These nouns are also known as mass nouns. They are usually used in the singular and without any article. They often needed counters to qualify them. Examples: (a bottle of) beer, (a cup of) rice, etc.

Collective nouns: They refer to persons, animals, or things in their groups. Example: Staff, team, committee, etc.

PRONOUN

Pronoun is etymologically derived from the Latin word "*pronomen*" which means "a name substituting for a name". It functions as a replacement of a noun. It beautifies our communication by saving us from repeating the use of a particular noun in a boring way.

There are several kinds of pronoun, and they include:

Personal Pronoun: They have special forms for gender, number, person and case. They refer to specific persons or things. Examples: He, She, It, I, We, They.

Possessive pronoun: It indicates ownership or possession; that is what belongs to someone. Examples: mine, yours, hers, his, ours, theirs, etc.

Reflexive Pronoun: This type of pronoun names a receiver of an action who is identical to the doer of the action. Examples: yourself, myself, himself, herself, itself, ourselves, yourselves, themselves.

Further example: Buhari congratulated himself on his fight for corruption. (Buhari is both the doer and the receiver of the action. He is the one congratulating himself.)

Indefinite pronoun: They refer to non-specific persons and things. Examples: Anybody, anyone, everybody, all, somebody, someone, something, nobody, everything, each one, either, neither, etc.

Interrogative pronoun: This is the pronoun that introduces questions. Examples: Whom, who, whose, what, which, etc.

VERB
A verb is popularly referred to as an action word. It generally expresses action or a state of being of the subject in a sentence. We can hardly explain any action without applying a verb.
Verbs are divided into:

Auxiliary verb: This is also known as a helping verb. Its major function is to support the main verb. Examples: Have, has, had, do, does, did, be, am, is, are, was, were, being, been, should, could, will, would, might, can, may, must, shall, etc.

Regular verb: These are verbs which derive their past tense and the past participle by the addition of the suffix "-ed", to the base. Example:
        Present infinitive: Pray.
        Present participle: Praying.
        Past tense: Prayed.
        Past participle: Prayed.

Irregular verbs: They are verbs whose formation is not constant. A lot of verbs in this category needed to be committed to the memory in order to make good use of them. However, one has to be careful especially when one is not sure of their different tenses. Example:

Present Infinitive	Past Tense	Past Participle
Rise	Rose	Risen
Lay (to place)	Laid	Laid
Lie (to recline)	Lay	Lain

ADVERB

An adverb is a word that modifies an action verb, an adjective or another adverb. It usually ends with "-ly", but this is not a strict rule, since some adjective can also end with "-ly".

There are other types of Adverb which include:

Adverb of Manner: This refers to how an action is done. Example: Ogechi *sang* wonderfully. ("Wonderfully" tells us how Ogechi *sang*.)

Adverb of Time: This tells us when something took place. Example: He came *last month*. ("Last month" indicates when he "came".)

Adverb of Place: This tells something about "where" something happens. Example: Well, I searched everywhere! ("everywhere" points to where I "searched".)

Adverb of Degree: This states the intensity to which a specific thing is done. Example: The man is very intelligent. ("very", tells us the degree of the man's intelligence.)

ADJECTIVE

An adjective modifies (describes) a noun or pronoun. It can specify the quality, the size, and the number of nouns or pronouns.

When Adjective is used as comparisons, if they are one or two syllables, "-er" is added (eg. bigger, faster, etc), but when they are longer than two syllables, "more" is used instead (eg. more beautiful, more intelligent, etc.).

When adjective is used as superlatives, if they are one or two syllables, "-est" is usually added (eg. the smartest, the greatest, etc.), but when they are longer than two syllables, "most" is used instead (eg. most beautiful, most intelligent, etc.).

PREPOSITION

They are linking words which show relationship between words especially in terms of possession, place, and time. It is usually placed before a noun or a pronoun, and they connect a noun or pronoun to another word in a sentence. Examples: since, with, down, from, up, without, in, with, for, by, off, beside, to, until, around, over, through, after, under, regarding, out, at, into, etc.

CONJUNCTION

This is a part of speech which joins words, phrases, or clauses together. There are two major types of conjunctions:

Coordinating conjunctions: They are words which join together, both logically and grammatically, elements of equal force. Examples: For, and, nor, but, or, yet, so.

Subordinating conjunction: They are words which join together, logically and grammatically, elements of unequal force by subordinating the lesser to the greater one. They join an independent clause to a subordinate clause. Examples: although, because, as if, after, before, since, unless, until, when, whenever, where, wherever, so that, though, while, etc.

INTERJECTION
These are words used to express emotional states. Since interjections are commonly used to convey strong emotions, they are usually followed by an exclamation point especially, if the emotional pitch is high. Since interjection has no grammatical relationship with other parts of the sentence, they could be removed without altering the meanings of the sentences. Examples:
Hurray, we won!
Wow! That's so nice of you.
Oh, That's great!

However, having discovered all these rudiments of speech, we are now better equipped to further our knowledge of speech delivery and how best to gain the attention of our audience in order to pass our message across. Speakers who have English as their second language should embark on regular practices and constantly build more vocabularies in order to be effective with the language of their speech.

CHAPTER SIX

HOW TO PRACTICE A SPEECH

Practice they say makes perfect. Anyone, who practices, is like one who spends a larger portion of his fortune in order to acquire a greater a fortune which he doesn't have. Practice makes a speech part and parcel of the speaker; it makes the speaker comfortable in answering any question arising from his speech.

However, for most of us, memorization of speeches is unnecessary – but practice is essential. The more familiar you become with your material, the easier the words flow. The more comfortable you feel with your words, the more naturally you present your speech. That explains why good speakers practice and practice again.[77] The beauty of the act of public speaking lies in the practice of the art. A good practice can be linked to Cicero's description that "to pass over the actual practice of eloquence – that governing force in every tranquil and free community – has nothing to compare with it, no impression more delightful than this can be received by the ear or the intelligence of man. Can any music be composed that is sweeter than a well-balanced speech? Is any poem better rounded than an artistic period in prose? What actor gives Keener Pleasure by his imitation of real life than your orator affords in his conduct of some real case? Does anything display more exact precision than a rapid succession of pointed reflections? Is there aught more wonderful than the lighting – up of a topic by verbal brilliance, or aught richer than a discourse furnished forth with material of every sort? And there is not a subject that is not the actor's own, provided it is one which deserves elegant and impressive treatment."[78]

There are many hints that can enable a person make a good practice in order to reproduce speeches with ease. To make a speech part and parcel of the speaker is the goal this chapter is set to achieve.

EFFORT AND COMMITMENT
The major problem in oratory is not having speech problem or impediments. The major problem is the assumption that speech impediments have no solution. There are two major ways to deal with speech impediment: firstly is by learning to live with it. And secondly is by putting a severe effort to improve on it.

LEARNING TO LIVE WITH SPEECH IMPEDIMENTS:
A speaker with speech impediments can better dispose his audience humorously about this impediment in order to save them from future distractions, tension and embarrassments. Thus Allen encourages, "what if you have an actual speech impediment or a physical problem that makes your voice sound odd? Does this mean you must forego the speech maker's art? No, it does not. I once interviewed a gentleman on television who had achieved remarkable success in the business world, even though he suffered from the condition known as harelip. TV interviewer Barbara Walters speaks with a slight lips. Talk-show host, Jack Paar had a severe stuttering problem as a young man. Author Truman Capote had an unfortunate voice intonation but was an interesting speaker nevertheless."[79] The ability to prepare a good speech, undergo as serious practices and knowing how to get the audience adapt to one's defects make the speaker great.

PUTTING A SEVERE EFFORT TO IMPROVE

There are many training formation that can enhance the ability to correct speech impediments. One can train oneself on how to save enough air in the lunge to speak. One can also learn through serious practices to improve his ability to pronounce and articulate words. An ambitious and enthusiastic orator no matter how bad a speech impediment is can make a big difference through a severe practice. Crassus advises such a person determined to improve his speaking conditions to press forward night and day in this single vocation, and do as the famous Athenian Demosthenes did, whose pre-eminence in oratory is unhesitatingly admitted, and whose zeal and exertions are said to have been such that at the very outset he surmounted natural drawbacks by diligent perseverance. Even though at first, he was shuttering so badly as to be unable to pronounce the initial R. of the art of his devotions, by practice he made himself accounted as distinct a speaker as anyone. Later on, though his breadth was rather short, he succeeded so far in making his breath hold during a speech, that a single oratorical period as his writings prove – covered two risings and two fallings of tone. Moreover, as the tale goes, it was his habit to slip pebbles in his mouth, and then declaim a number of verses at the top of his voice and without drawing breadth, and this not only as he stood still, but while walking about, or going up a steep slope.[80]

Thus, the effort put into this mode of improving speaking skill is great and can only be achieved by able and determined persons. A speaker must have an inner motivation which should be a towing van drawing him towards the part of perfection in speaking.

LEARNING THE PROPER WAY OF IMITATION

In as much as John Mason would have it that 'imitation is limitation', a sensible imitation can do: if you don't have courage to speak, imitate those who have. If you don't have a method of delivery, imitate those who have better ones. If you don't know how to pronounce words well, imitate those who can pronounce well. If you don't have a nice accent, change location to places with nice accent or you can imitate those who have nice accents. Allen captures this idea succinctly when he says: "probably the best method of all is to at least tone down an accent, if it is of the objectionable sort, is to pay careful attention to those radio and television voices that are obviously in the pleasant-to-hear category."[81] Examples are people like: Cyril Stober, Euginia Abu, Walter Cronkite, Diane Sawyer, Kierian Umeayo, Dan Rather, Morley Safer, Mike Wallace, George Will, Joyce Unaegbu, or other newscasters, actors, or entertainers with great and attractive speaking style.

Furthermore, in trying to copy or imitate others, the speaker should avoid copying the negative or faulty ones, because faults are easily copied. It is also advised that after copying, a serious practice should follow in order to know how well you can manage what you have copied. Cicero supported this view when he said: "let practice be added, whereby in copying he may reproduce the pattern of his choice and not portray him as time and again I have known many copyists do, who in copying hunt after such characteristics as are easily copied or even abnormal and possibly faulty. For nothing is easier than to imitate a man's style of dress, pose or gaits. Moreover, if there is a fault, it is not much trouble to appropriate that and to copy it ostentatiously."[82]

PRACTICE HOW TO WRITE

Psychologists have discovered that the ability to write down something makes the learning of that particular thing easier. Those things we write will be unconsciously recording somewhere in our mind that once we are about to memorize, they easily come out on their own; writing helps quicker articulation. Any orator who cannot write is handicapped. This is because even if you don't need to read your speech from a written text, your can write speech and then glance at it once in a while to remember what to say. Good Orators write some words with emphasis so that during their delivery, once they set their eyes on the text, they see the emphasized words and come to remember what they might have forgotten.

More so, practicing written speeches guide the speaker throughout the speech to maintain his style and to avoid derailing from the focus of his speech. These are the things which in good orators produce applause and admiration; and no man will attain these, except by long and large practice in writing. He may have trained himself in those off-hand declamations; he too who approaches oratory by way of long practice in writing, brings this advantage to his task, that even if he is extemporizing, whatever he may say bear a likeness to the written word. If ever during the speech, he has introduced a written note, the rest of his discourse, when he turns away from the note, will proceed in unchanged style.[83] Hence, good orators are good managers of their manuscripts.

PRACTICE MEMORISING RELEVANT THINGS

It is advised to memorize some relevant parts of your speech. You can memorize the first two or three sentences of your speech or the last two or three sentences of your speech conclusion. You can also try to memorize relevant quotations should in case you wish to quote verbatim. You can also memorize words with special emphasis, or words that are foreign to the audience. This orator's business of memorizing can only be achieved through continuous rehearsal, so you are advised to practice and practice as much as you can.

But the problem of speech practice is usually lack of sufficient practice or rehearsal, and another problem is trying to memorize the whole pages of the work. Some experts on the art of public speaking however, are horrified by the very prospect of memorizing a speech. Art Linkletter, for example, states his feeling plainly enough: 'you should never, never, try to memorize an entire speech word-for-word'.

THE DOS AND DONTS IN PRACTICING YOUR SPEECH

There are a lot of things that the speaker needs to put into consideration when practicing a speech. Know it that for a speaker to be able to study and reproduce a speech perfectly is not enough. There are also some non-verbal techniques the knowledge of which will be relevant for an effective delivery. The ability to make a good delivery starts from the final day of practices or rehearsal; you can always discover this yourself. There are also some unconscious bad habits a speaker might have developed without knowing that such habits serve as a distraction to the audience. That is why the list of the 'dos' and 'don't' are enumerated below to enable a speaker tutor his or herself through these dos and don'ts. Here are the dos and don'ts:[84]

DOS!

❖ Go to the room where you will give your presentation to get a feel for the environment /set-up.

- ❖ Practice in front of a friends without stopping, just as you will want to give your presentation on speech day.

- ❖ Practice in front of a mirror (full length if possible).

- ❖ Practice using visual aids so you know how much time they will take up and how to incorporate them into your speech.

- ❖ Practice with background and noise (is-turn on the TV, radio, etc.) in order to practice with distractions.

- ❖ Practice with the actual speech outline you will use in your presentation.

- ❖ Practice your speech dressed as you plan to be for your actual presentation so that you can fail comfortable and ready to speak.

- ❖ Time yourself -- make sure that you are consistently within your time frame.

- ❖ Video tape yourself if possible. This is the best way for you to be able to see what your mistakes are so that you can fix them before you give your presentation.

- ❖ Practice becoming aware of your posture and mannerisms as you speak. If you are going to use movement on speech day -- you need to practice moving --keep it controlled and natural.

- ❖ Eliminate any distracting mannerisms you may have. Distracting mannerisms include (but are not limited to) many nervous habits you might have (live, playing with a ring or necklace, tucking hair behind your ear, playing with a pen, cracking knuckles, etc.). These are actions you can easily avoid doing if you are aware of them.

DON'TS

- ❖ Never have change or keys in your pockets. You do not want to have the sound of objects competing with your voice.

- ❖ Never wear a hat, unless it is part of your presentation. Dress appropriately any time you give a presentation. It is better to make a credible first impression by looking as if you are interested in giving a good speech.

- ❖ Do not use distracting mannerisms.

- ❖ Do not stand with your arms crossed or your hands in your pockets. This type of posture prevents you from gesturing and may even make your audience uncomfortable.

- ❖ Never apologize if you make a mistake while giving a speech. Simple correct the mistake and move on. You never want to draw light to an error, chance are most people will miss it anyway. Along these same lines, never make faces when you make a mistake, it is better to just keep going.

- ❖ Don't put your visual aids up in front of the class before you explain them. Rather introduce them as you are speaking. Also, don't keep visual aids up after you are no longer referring to them. Use Visual Cues on your speaking outline to easily avoid these blunders.

❖ Don't practice your speech holding on to your outline. When you are practicing put your outline on something – Music stand; A box: A high counter, anything to simulate the lectern that you will be presenting with.

The Art of Oratory

CHAPTER SEVEN

HOW TO MEMORISE YOUR SPEEH

Memory is the capacity of reproducing in consciousness different experiences that belonged to it previously but which had become unconscious. Memory always implies a relation to time.[85] It is also the proof of having learned, through recalling what has been learnt off-hand. Memory broadens our world, and helps us manage trio-consciousness (past, present, and future) of our world. Without memory, we would lack the sense of continuity and at the beginning of each day encounter ourselves and things around us as strangers. Each day and event would exist in isolation; it would be impossible to either infer from the past or anticipate the future.

The human brain weighs about 1.4 kilograms and is roughly the size of a grapefruit, yet it contains some 100 billion neurons, or nerve cells, all of which form an incredibly complex network. Indeed, just one neuron may be connected to 100 others. This writing gives the brain the potential to process and retain (memorize) a vast amount of information.[86] Memory is the pivot around which a lot of mental activities revolve. It is very useful when one comes to speech delivery. A lot of audiences are turned off or become allergic to written speeches, but pay more attention when it is extemporized. Thus Bishop Fulton Sheen once recalled the remark of an old Irish woman concerning a Bishop who was reading a speech: "Glory be to God, if he can't remember it, how does he expect us to?" he further says, "*I learned the lecture from the inside out, not from the outside in....* I would write out from memory my recollection of the points."[87]

Only people with powerful memory can know what they are going to say and for how long they are going to speak and in what style, what points they have already answered and what still remains; and they also can remember from other cases many arguments which they have previously advanced and many which they have heard from other people.[88] Memory involves three stages: encoding, storage, and retrieval. Your brain encodes information when it perceives it and registers it. This information can then be stored for future retrieval. Memory failure occurs when any one of these stage breaks down.

There are so many ways one can memorize: constant practices or the system of read, understand, and read again can do. But the sense of sight and hearing can do more favor to the mind and memory for better reproduction of learned activities. But since the levels and methods of memorizing differ in individuals, orators as the champions in matters of memory should know their capacity, so as to know how to prepare for effective delivery. Hence, Cicero observes, '… a memory for thing is the special property of the orator."[89]

USE OF MNEMONICS:
Mnemonics is applied to memory aids, used as far back as Greek and Roman antiquity. Simonides of Ceos was said to be the first who invented the science of mnemonics. A story has it that Simonides while dining at the house of a wealthy nobleman named Scopas at Crannon in Thessaly, chanted a lyric Poem which he had composed in honor of his host, in which he followed the Custom of the Poets by including for decorative purposes a long passage referring to Castor and Pollux; whereupon Scopas with excessive meanness told him

he would pay him half the fee agreed on for the Poem, and if he liked he might apply for the balance to his sons of Tyndarous, as they had gone halves in the Panegyric. The story runs that a little later a message was brought to Simonides to go outside, as two young men were standing at the door who earnestly requested him to come out; so he rose from his seat and went out, and could not see anybody; but in the interval of his absence the roof of the hall where Scopes was giving the Banquet fell in, crushing Scopas himself and his relations underneath the ruins and killing them; and when their friends wanted to bury them but were altogether unable to know them apart as they had been completely crushed, the story goes that Simonides was enabled by the recollection of the place in which each of them had been reclining at table to identify them for separate interment; and that this circumstance suggested to him the discovery of the truth that the best aid to clearness of memory consists in orderly arrangement.[90]

There are various kinds of mnemonics. The most popular consist of verses formed from the material to be memorized. In each mnemonic device, an additional indexing cue is memorized along with the material to be learned.

SOME POPULAR MNEMONIC DEVICES

Method of loci:
The word Loci is a Latin word for "Places". This is the oldest popular mnemonic device which works well for al list of 10-15 items mentally placed in a series of logically connected places. For example: If you want to remember people, you may begin to think about the man sitting in the front seat, the man that stood on the door, the man sitting on the back seat.

Experience shows that this is a very effective method of memorizing.

Acronym method:
These are words formed from the first letter of a group of words. Acronym leads to the use of initial in dealing with names and other related things. For instance: UNESCO - United Nations Educational Scientific and Cultural Organization.

Another system of acronym is the use of the first words of sentences to form a more familiar sentence in order to enable you remember what you are about to memorize. Example: Williams Hates Obinna, can represent World Health Organization (WHO). Whenever this phrase is remembered, they quicken the rate at which we remember the real thing we wish to memorize.

Keyboard Method:
This is the act of memorizing what is meaningful and understandable. It is easy to memorize what has meaning than what has no meaning. Even if the words about to be memorized have no meaning, try to give them meaning, so as to make them easy to be remembered. Experience proves that greater number of people learn through this method, only few can memorize things they don't understand.

INDIVIDUAL DIFFERENCES IN MEMORISING
Every individual is unique in his or her ability to memorize and these individual differences form the basis of the different kinds of memory. It is relevant to know where you belong and also learn to improve yourself. Here are the various patterns of memory.

Rote Memory:
This memory pattern is measured by tests of learning to repeat verbatim a group of meaningless words. Rote memory is often studied with respect to the number of repetitions necessary to learn a selection to the point where one perfect reproduction can be given immediately afterwards.

Meaningful Memory:
It is measured by measures of recall of passage the subject reads, hears, or memorizes. In meaningful memory the words and sentences are categorized into ideas, which are frequently remembered even though the specific words that give rise to them may be forgotten.

Ideational or Logical Memory:
Here, intellectual operations are involved, and the procedure of course is different. People with logical memory cannot understand any topic unless it has some logical connection. Their memory is a friend to coherent and consistent sentences or statements.

Visual Memory:
They are usually good in identifying or distinguishing objects and events, and retain their memory at heart. They have an extraordinary capacity of sight-seeing. They hardly forget whatever they see with their eyes and remember exactly the way such things are.

Motor Memory:
People with such memory are good in remembering series of exercises like gymnastic. The Asians are champions in this memory pattern because they are much gifted with the ability to memorize reflex actions.

Laud Memory:
People with laud memory usually have a kind of brain which only learns by shouting or reading out the words loudly. They read aloud at studies. Majority of those that belong to this group are the learned in the society.

Acoustic Memory:
They are people who have the high ability to differentiate sounds and rhythm. They are mainly the great musicians in the society.

Number Memory:
They are good in memorizing numbers and they can code information with numbers for easy retention. They are mostly good in mathematics and Sciences, and are also good in remembering dates.

Verbal Memory:
People with verbal memory naturally possess a high power of articulation. Once they learn words, the words remain; they have a good work book.[91]

Color Memory:
They memorizes with colors. They are usually color conscious and can easily differentiate similar colors from another.

Eidetic Memory:
A lot of children are good at this memory pattern, but at adulthood when they begin to engage in abstract thinking most of them lose this ability. Only about 2% of any given population has eidetic memory. They don't study much. Their mere browsing through the note in a short period can merit them a verbatim recitation of the note. They are sometimes referred to as people with a photographic memory. However, they are mostly the geniuses in the

society and they need little studies to memorize accurately.[92]

THEORIES OF RETENTION
These theories describe the mechanism of forgetting. The theories are not contradicting in any way at all; they might rather differ primarily in the phenomena observed and in the approaches which the investigator applies to the study of forgetting. These theories include:

Interference Theory:
This theory is really a collection of notions which describe the forgetfulness arising from interfering memories. The basic mechanism is that we forget one item because another item interferes by taking its place.

Decay Theory:
It states simply that as a function of the ravages of time memories fade away. We tend to forget a lot of information we have gathered after a long period of time and development. As a result of lack of utility or usage, the information decays and is forgotten.

Motivated-Forgetting Theory:
This theory is not generally applied except to situations of complex and relatively severe existing motivations. The fundamental notion is one that derives from Freudian personality theory and concerns the mechanism called repression. Memories are repressed when their recall would evoke great unpleasantness for the individual.

The Displacement Theory:
A hypothesis that is related with interference is one which says that the memory store has a limited capacity and thus any separate input to it will eliminate or displace items that are already there. It there is no new information overtime

then no forgetfulness will occur.

The Loss Access:
Actually you don't forget anything, but the things you seem to have forgotten have merely become temporally inaccessible for one thing or the other. In other words, all the information is there in the memory where they are stored, but has become inaccessible because of the retrieval cues.

Current Appraisal:
Aristotle is the originator of this theory. This is a theory of memory and forgetfulness that lays emphasis on the importance of contiguity and contrast. But this theory has not produced any experimental research that will help us explain the aspect of forgetting.

THE LAWS OF LEARNING[93]

A lot of influencing factors either help or hinder learning. These influences have been discovered by experimental psychologists over the years. The statements of these influences are commonly referred to as the laws of learning. They include the laws of intensity, organization, contiguity, exercise, effect, facilitation, and interference.

The Law of Intensity:
This states that the rate of learning depends on the strength of the response to the stimulus situation.

The Law of Organization:
This states that learning is more rapid when material is organized into meaningful relationships.

The Law of Contiguity:
This states that in order for association to occur, the associated events must fall within a certain time limit. For

instance: in some sequential acts like memorizing poems, each part becomes connected to the part performed just before it, which is contiguous in time.

The Law of Exercise:
This states that the performance of an act, under conditions favorable to learning, tends to make subsequent performance of the act easier.

The Law of Effect:
This states that a response leading to a satisfying result is likely to be learned, while a response leading to an annoying result is likely to be extinguished. The idea of satisfaction here means to fulfill some need or motive of the individual in the learning situation.

Some psychologists prefer the idea of *reinforcement* to the idea of effect, pointing out that unsatisfactory consequences can be as effective in response selection as satisfactory consequences if they are vivid, novel, or striking.

The Laws of Facilitation and of Inference:
This states that one act of learning will assist another act of learning if some stimuli in the new situation need a response already associated with them in the old situation, but will hinder the new act of learning if a stimulus which needed a single response in the old situation now needs a different response in the new situation.

EFFICIENCY LEARNING AND REMEMBERING
Having the Intention to Remember:
Reading with the intention of remembering influences our ability to learn and determines the direction which learning will take. A person cannot efficiently learn and recall accurately without having the intention to learn. This

intention to learn involves commitment to the process. Experiment has shown that even intelligent people also find it difficult to recall what they have learnt many times uninterestingly.

Whole Learning:
It is usually very effective to learn as a whole. This is because learning as a whole or integrally, helps you to learn things that have meaning so that the meaning will be systematic when you try to recall them, rather than learning partly, which makes the learned information confusing. A popular saying holds that 'half knowledge is dangerous'.

Recitation:
Recitation facilitates the ability to remember or toe store information. When you read and recite you find those words gradually register in your memory and ever ready to be recalled. This is workable at all age levels. The value of this method appears to result from the following factors: (a) In reciting, you are necessarily active and alert; (b) By reciting and prompting yourself with the printed material, you can discover your mistakes and correct them before recitation on the stage; (c) In reciting, you are studying as you will later have to perform – answering questions; (d) Recitation provides you with an immediate goal for achievement.[94]

Distributed Practice:
Remembering improves if you review each subject for some time each day in addition to reviewing it just before public delivering long-time retention is favored by such spacing of study. Shorter learning periods are conducive to more intensive work; and when a subject is uninteresting, this is often the only way you can learn it at all.

Imitation:
A careful observation of a model helps the learner to reproduce well. Human beings have the tendency and ability to learn by imitation. But imitated act has to be put into practice to ensure effective learning and careful elimination of mistakes.

Knowledge of Results:
Mirroring back to our past record and performance offers us an incentive to improve the more. People of higher self-esteem are stronger in competition and use this medium to improve themselves.

Survey:
Any form of learning in man is just like adding some blocks to the already existing foundation. We learn and store information on the existed ones. Therefore, the more information we have on a topic the easier for us to learn new things about that particular topic. Apart from reading books like novel that have no table of content, survey method encourages you to survey first the table of content so that you can have little information about what you are to know better when you start to read. It is also advised to skim session and look at illustration too since they also facilitate learning.

Review:
This process follows after reading and reciting. For the purpose of retaining the information, you are advised to continue to recite for a very long time to enable you correct your mistake and to make the work part of you before you can publicly deliver the work. There are many important gains of review, among them are: (a) it helps you avoid error (b) it helps to avoid tension during presentation (c) it makes the presentation flow naturally form you. (d) it makes you feel at home with the information you are about to deliver.

Question:

A lot of people avoid asking themselves questions after reading because for them, a person who has memorized something should not talk in order not to forget what has been memorized. But questions enable you to face the challenge of answering any question from the information you just learnt. Questions will also help you to know your information very well such that even if you tend to forget few things in it, you will be able to paraphrase or explain certain things from what you've learnt off-hand.

CHAPTER EIGHT

HOW TO DELIVER YOUR SPEECH

A lot of people make a useless assumption by thinking that speech delivery is only all about words of a speech or the verbal aspect of a speech. This assumption is faulty because, without the addition of another aspect of speech delivery, which is nonverbal in nature, a speech will be monotonous and therefore sustenance of interest will be at stake. This chapter is aimed at exposing to a considerable extent the goal of both verbal and non-verbal aspects of communication. It will also show how a synthesis of both verbal and non-verbal communication can make a speech presentation more wonderful than an application of only one aspect of communication.

NONVERBAL AND VERBAL COMMUNICATION
Verbal communication is done orally. It is a vocal production of words; it is basically made up of words which form meaning. Words are spoken to generally suit the ordinary meanings of the words or the new meanings given to the words by the speaker to suit his purpose. The meaning of words in verbal communication is also regulated by the rules of grammar and syntax or in accordance with language games. This aspect of communication is much clearer to a native speaker but can also be learned.

The Nonverbal aspects of speech delivery are the direct opposite of the verbal. It is a type where actions can speak to the understanding of people. Albeit, it is a delicate aspect of speech delivery because it can sometimes vary from culture to culture. It basically governs our actions far from words during speech delivery.

However, the scope of the nonverbal delivery is so wide that it is difficult to explore. New patterns, new features are often discovered everyday so as to complement and supplement any deficiency in this aspect of communication.

Moreover, the verbal and nonverbal aspects of speech delivery can effectively work in *pari passu* with each other for a greater output. But when they work against each other, the revers is the case. The effective combination of verbal and nonverbal communication in speech making is natural, and make for a better communication. "When they work together, what we communicate nonverbally serves to repeat, complement, substitute for, or in some way regulates what we say verbally. For example, if we say, "Get out!" and point to the door, we are repeating; if we spread our hands and arms while describing a panorama in front of us, we merely shrug our shoulders in reply, we are substituting; if we avoid eye contact because we do not want to speak to someone (or vice versa; if we catch his eye because we do), we are regulating."[95]

In either way, when the verbal and nonverbal work together in opposition to each other when they contradict each other, there occurs a state of anarchy in communication, where the actual meaning is scrambled for. The law of contradiction states that something cannot be and be at the same time. So, one cannot keep moving his head up and down, which means "yes" while verbally saying "No". It is impossible and even when possible does not make a good sight.

Sometimes the actions in the nonverbal communication are unconsciously displayed; they are so inbuilt that we might not need to practice what we sign before we represent them.
They are very apt in translating the verbal message directly into action or in representing directly, the inner feelings of a speaker. This is where crime dictators take the advantage for truth discovery. Example when one is saying that one is ignorant of a crime while at the same time fidgeting, it means that the culprit might be lying since what he/she is saying (verbally) contradicts his/her actions (nonverbally).

Consequently, it is evidently clear that the nonverbal aspect of communication does not communicate everything that the verbal can communicate. For instance, a deaf and dumb person finds it very difficult to communicate everything including his inner feelings and ideas but the reverse is the case in verbal communication. Litfin observes that the reason for this is because nonverbal communication channels are especially well adapted to communicating attitudes, feelings, and relationships rather than cognitive information.[96]

PHYSICAL DELIVERY/NONVERBAL COMMUNICATION

The physical aspect of speech delivery also has a very important role to play in a speech presentation, but have a lot of complications associated with it. A particular kind of physical delivery can sometimes be deemed reasonable in a particular culture, but might have negative connotation in another. Physical delivery generally has a great impact on the outcome of an orator's performance, therefore an in-depth study of culture, sensitivity of the environment and consciousness of the speaker/orator will help to clear the rainy cloud for public speakers. Here are some delicate parts of the physical delivery which will be fairly treated here:

body movements, eye contact, facial expressions, physical appearance, and the use of space.

Body Movements:
This involves those significant movements of speakers during delivery, which have a lot of meaning to communicate to the audience. Such movements involve: gestures, postures, etc.

The body movement of a speaker is extremely sensitive. Some audiences get biased about a speaker right from the very moment the speaker enters the stage. They are prompted to draw hasty conclusions and assumptions about a speaker especially when the speaker is foreign to the audience. That is why you should be in control of your attitude before your audience. Much is expected from you. They would ask: are you in control of the situation or rather frightened and nervous? Do you stand tall, or are you slouching? Is there certain dignity to the way you sit, or do you sag into your chair like a sack of flour? When you walk to the podium, do you do so with strength and vigor, or do you move with reluctance like someone facing an execution? Do you hold your head high, or let it drop low as if you are fearful of catching someone's eye? All of these things and more are eagerly examined by your listeners to see what sort of person you are."[97] Sensitivity matters a lot on the part of any good public speaker when it comes to matters of nonverbal communication.

Gestures:
According to some researchers, the human body is capable of displaying about 700,000 different gestures which can be instrumental in communicating meaning to audience. Every motion of a speaker during presentation should be regulated so and also in conformity with the verbal content of the

speech; gestures should flow in synchrony with the meaning of the words spoken.

Although gestures should be regulated against excesses, it is encouraged that it should be spontaneous so as to make it natural. This is because the contemporary audience delights more in things that are homely or natural, rather than artificial. Speakers are warned not to exceed limits in matters of gestures or repeat a particular gesture always, lest it breeds a big distraction.

In matters of gestures, there is no rule that regulates the particular gesture which much be used at a particular time. This is because the presence of such a rule can render a delivery stereotypic in nature and thus lead the audience into predicting gestures for speakers. Gestures should be applied according to the particular speaker at a particular time. Popular speakers are sometimes known and are associated by their unique kind of gestures.

However, gestures are also applied according to the culture of the audience because they vary from one culture to another, or from one region to another, "for instance Americans and most Europeans understand the thumbs-up gesture to mean "all right," but in Southern Italy and Greece, it transmits the message for which we reserve the middle finger. Making a circle with the thumb and the forefinger is friendly in the United States, but it means "you're worth zero" in France and Belgium; it is a vulgar sexual invitation in Greece and Turkey. The best advice for the foreign traveller is to leave gestures at home."[98] Good speakers are quick to study the gestures of a particular culture they are to deliver their speeches. The use of a wrong gesture or the application of gesture which is foreign to the audience breeds one of the highest distractions in speech delivering.

Gestures which are mostly, the movement of head and hand, are the most signalers of meaning. The sign that makes up these gestures can be classified under "emblems" and "adaptors".

- ❖ **Emblem:** These are gestures that are symbolic – they have direct meaning in words. They are universal signs and once applied everyone knows the meaning. For example, when there is noise by the audience and the speaker raises his hand with the fingers together and the palm open. This means that the speaker is saying that everyone should keep quiet.

- ❖ **Illustrators:** These are gestures that are descriptive in nature. Example: when a speaker raises one of his hands up and uses the other hand to hold it at any length and the outstretched hand to illustrate the length of a snake. He can say, 'the snake is as tall as this my hand".

- ❖ **Adaptors:** These refer to gestures that take the place of stress. Adaptors are safety valves that jettison unwanted stress.[99] Tensions go with public speaking, and these tensions are sometimes so great that if not channelled to another thing they may constitute a huge distraction to the speaker. The stress can manifest when the speaker begins to march one leg on the ground, when the speaker stands with the hands behind the back, he might begin to sweat, blink the eye and exhibit similar behaviours. These adaptors are gestures that are very much natural and sometimes lie beyond the speaker's control.

Eye Contact:
There are up to twenty-three separate and distinct eyebrow positions that communicate different meanings. The role of the eye during speech delivery is very significant such that it is impossible to be neglected. In some cultures (like North America) eye contact is so important that it is taken as a basic prerequisite for effective take off during speech delivery. Albert the importance of eye contact varies from culture to culture and requires extreme sensitivity when applied.

Eye contact serve as an automatic sole regulator of verbal communication in the sense that once you stare into somebody's eye, communication is initiated immediately. If you stare a person into the eyes and the person stares in return, it signals a welcome, but if the person refuses to stare back and rather decides to look at other direction, it means a sign of disinterestedness. That is why we are scarred most often talking with people wearing dark eye glasses because it is difficult to read their eyes.

In public speaking, audiences are so conscious of the speakers' eyes that once they refuse to make contact, they see the speaker as one talking to himself or as one who doesn't care about his audience. "When I first started speaking" Sherman admitted, "I had trouble looking into the eyes of my listeners. I'd stare at my notes, glance at my audiovisuals and peer into the distance – as if the audience was somewhere else. On my early evaluation forms, the same advice kept appearing. "Establish more eye contact" I made that adjustment."[100]

It is thus clear that, "Good eye contact between speaker and audience promotes effective communication; poor eye contact hinders effective communication. Since the choice of whether to have good or poor eye contact is almost entirely up to the speaker, and since the matter is such an important one, the practice of good eye contact deserves and receives a major emphasis."[101]

Avoid the outdated rule of looking at the fringe of your audience hair as it defiles an effective communication. "The best way to maintain eye contact is by looking directly at a single member of the audience for two or three seconds (no longer than that, or the person will think that you are staring) and then moving on to look at someone eyes in the pattern of an "M" or "W" and then switching over to an "X" pattern is a good way of appearing random in your eye movements,"[102] but this system can only be effective when there are few persons in the audience. In a case of a larger audience, divide the audience mentally into different sections and from time to time, look at particular sections without focusing on a particular individual for some seconds, and then turn to look at another section.

A continuous practice will make these principles stick to the speaker's consciousness or the speaker might adopt the nine eye-opening keys of Sherman: Don't talk to your notes or to your visual aids, start seeing friends, use the three-second rule, look at many, not a few, don't worry about large groups, practice making your eyes expressive and look for feedback.[103] All these enable you to engage your audience, and the audience will in turn appreciate the fact that you are friendly and caring to them, it is then that they will offer you the right decorum you needed.

Facial Expressions:
The face is a delicate part to handle by a speaker during speech delivery. This is because audiences are fond of looking at the face of the speaker always in order to know the speakers mood or frame of mind at the moment. The face

according to researchers is capable of displaying an estimate of 500,000 or more different meaningful expressions.

Once you look at the face of a speaker, common sense can easily discern those basic feelings of a speaker such as when he is happy, angry, lying, terrified, etc. One of the basic mistakes speakers make is to take the audience for granted, thinking that the audience are so foolish that they can manipulate them by masking their facial expression – pretending to be intoxicated with laugh when indeed you are not disposed to laugh, pretending to feel pity about something when indeed you are displaying no emotion of pity either. You are advised to be closer to your audience and your face will always enhance your speech. Facial expression serves as an elucidifier to the speech you make. It helps you express your attitudes and feelings about the topic you are treating.

Finally, Duane gave a general rule which I consider as a *modus operandi* for effective facial management, "… try to maintain a relaxed, pleasant expression. Sometimes you will be lighthearted and humorous; depending on what you are saying at the moment. But through al of the kaleidoscope changes of facial expression, try to allow your facial muscles to remain relaxed, unstrained, and pleasant to look at. Tight jaws, narrowed eyes, flared nostrils, furrowed brow-all of these typically represent forms of hostility, anger, strain, and frustration, none of which should characterize the speaker (except on certain limited occasions)."[104]

Physical Appearance:
Audiences have a way of deciphering smart, dull, humorous, arrogant and other characters in speakers only by the way a speaker appears the first time to an audience. Experience also proves that a higher percentage of the assumptions people

make about speakers' physical appearance are usually true. "We constantly communicate to one another by the way we clothe and groom our bodies. We can present ourselves formally, neatly or sloppily, modestly or provocatively, expensively or cheaply, in good taste or poor taste, or in any combination thereof And as we do so, people who see us make inferences about our personality and abilities."[105]

Speakers are advised to dress up in conformity with the words being communicated. If you want your audience to see you as gentle, dress gently. If you want them to see you as a jester, dress to attract laughter. You are what you dress. Sometime ignorant speakers make the mistake of wearing clothes with odd inscriptions – a person talking on "how to be a good Christian" wearing clothe written "I'm very sexy" is very odd and quite contrary to the message being communicated.

For the purpose of avoiding mistake, speakers are advised to dress in a very plain color. An extreme combination of colors (color rioting) distracts the focus of your audience and even irritates their sentiments.

In the situation where the orator is facing dressing decision problem, buying the idea of Sherman will do. "Men: wear a white or blue dress shirt (not button-down) and a "quiet" tie. Dress one level "above" your audience. You can dress more informally if it is a casual event, but your clothes should always be fastidiously pressed and classy. Women: wear solid dresses or "officer" suits. Avoid excessive jewelry, makeup or extreme hair styles. Try wearing 'jewel tone" jackets and black shirts for a combination of power and energy."[106]

THE USE OF SPACE:
This is a vast area of study in public speaking. Naïve and novice speaker complicate a lot of issues in matters of space. Some on the bid to gain comfort or authority dabble into creating a psychological problem in audience. Audiences are friends to embrace and should be handled with care. Speakers are expected to watch on the Elevation, distance and to avoid obstruction during delivery.

Elevation:
In most halls or places of speech delivery, podiums or stages are often built to the advantage of the speaker. Once a speaker mounts on a higher platform, the audience is already intimidated by the height of the speaker, they therefore see the speaker as somebody higher than them and sometimes as someone unapproachable. The opposite is the amphitheaters where the speaker is below the audience. Only an experienced speaker can stand such intimidating position of the audience.

In places with high podiums, speakers are advised to avoid mounting on them when the audiences are few. Only a large audience can make a speaker mount a podium, but some pertinent points should be communicated outside the podiums.

Distance:
Everybody needs acceptance and abhors rejection. Sometimes, the ability to discover when neglected or accepted is innate in us. Audience wants their relationship with the speaker to be a sort of tête-à-tête. When the speaker is far from them, they tend psychologically to see the speaker as one very standoffish or as one trying to keep them at arm's length. Moreover, the problem of distance sometimes varies depending on culture. "North Americans tend to be more

defensive about space than members of some other cultures."[107]

For speaker to create a form of intimacy, he would have to leave the stage and embrace the audience – coming closer to them. He would have to bridge the gap which hangs psychologically somewhere in the unconscious minds of listeners. The speaker can begin to work around the audience's sitting position but not to the extent of causing distractions. When the audience is not sitting so close to the first pews, the speaker can then re-locate to the first row so as to be nearer to the people.

Thus, the ability to accept the audience as friends and companions solves a heavy deal of the problem of distance.

Obstructions:
These are psychological or physical opaque walls between the speaker and the audience. Sometimes, these walls are built consciously or unconsciously by the speaker or even by the nature of the building where the speech is being delivered.

Some flowers, Lecterns, stages, sound speakers etc are so built or arranged so much so that they do more harm than good.

The speaker is the center of attraction and therefore, the audience should be given the right full eye-access to the speaker. Any kind of shade separating the speaker from the audience serves as a barrier and hindrance to effective communication. It is advised that the speaker should make the choice of speaking from a transparent lectern or a shorter one. Sound-speakers should be given the right position and the quest for aesthetics should not be antagonistic to effective delivery.

UNITS AND PROCESSES OF SPEECH:

Speeches are not as a result of an unorganized way of producing sound without any method or rules. There is a method of producing speech sounds and there are other parts, internal and external parts that help to produce sounds through the vocal tract.

In speaking, tongue, lips, and jaws are moved, and then a column of air from the lungs is expelled. These rapid movements change the shape of the oral and nasal cavities through which sound resonates after air passes over our vocal cords. The result is the production of different sounds. In the production of a vowel sound, the tongue is held at such a distance from the roof of the mouth that there is no perceptible frictional noise, while in producing a consonant, the tongue is help very close to the roof of the mouth and voiced air-stream of ordinary force is emitted and a frictional noise is heard in addition to the voice.

Furthermore, there is variation in the number of distinct speech sounds depending on language. The sounds are known as 'Phonemes' (sounds, which are used to distinguish one word from another). The English language has about 45 phonemes, Hawaiian language about 13 and so on. The uses of phonemes are dependent upon language, because they change as the language changes.

Phonemes are organized into morphemes (the smallest language unit that possesses meaning). Morphemes are organized into words, and words are organized into sentences in order to express different thoughts. "By keeping within the constraints of these rules, an inexhaustible supply of speech is possible. This is what gives our language its incredible flexibility and diversity."[108]

Rate:
It refers to the speed or frequency upon which a speech is made. A speaker is advised to speak faster when delivering a speech, this is because some speakers most often make a useless assumption that the best way of delivering is speaking at the lowest pace and therefore, they fall into the problem of boring their audience with their speeches. 'When you slow your speech down you are giving the audience twice the mental time needed to receive the message. Most audience members will take this excess time and use it to daydream."[109] The average speed of speech falls between the range of 120 to 160 words per minute and researches have also proved that listening and thinking can take place four times faster than that of speaking.

Some speakers on the other hand, make the mistake of speaking fast to the extent of muttering some incomprehensible words. It is encouraged that even though you need to speed up your speech, you should also make sure you are able to articulate clearly and speak clearly. "Don't speak so fast that you tripping over your words. The rate should be comfortable for you. But always remember that you need to speak with a degree of urgency – get to your point."[110]

Monotony in anything leads to boredom. Good speakers should avoid monotone throughout a particular delivery. It is good to vary the voice rate at every interval of the delivery depending on what the speaker is about to communicate. The speech should start at a considerable slow pace and continue is a uniform acceleration unless where the points need to be pointed out emotionally or forcefully which might call for a different pace. Hence, it is also good to end a speech with a faster rate. Such diversities garnish a speech an enable it to keep the audience spellbound till the end.

The varieties in voice parts in music – base, soprano, alto and tenor result from differences in pitch. Some voices naturally or artificially are of a higher pitch while others fall at a lower pitch. These matter a lot when delivering a speech.

Pitch basically refers to the degree of highness or lowness of voice which is quite different from volume. The pitches of the voice of a speaker have many things to communicate to the audience about how interesting a particular speech can be; it determines the level of enthusiasm and acceptability that will follow your speech.

A speaker with a very high pitch or those with an extremely lower pitch make little impression to their audience. It is encouraged that speakers should keep inflecting their pitches to avoid shouting or boring down the psychology of their audience. Among the major problems of speakers here is the inability to exhibit much energy in their vocal presentation. But a serious practice and training can bring about the best in the speaker. Thus Cicero maintains that, "no devoted of eloquence will become, by my advice, a slave to his voice, after the manner of the Greek tragedians, who both for many a year practice declamation from their chairs, and every day, before their performance on the stage, lie down and gradually raise the voice, and later, after playing their part. Take their seats, and bring it back again from the highest treble to the lowest bass, and in a way regain control of it I once more encourage practice, practice".[111]

Volume:
The volume is the lowness and loudness of a voice when speaking. Speakers are encouraged to always speak aloud. One of the greatest punishments a speaker can give to his audience is to speak in a lower voice, thereby stressing the

audience' ear as they attempt to comprehend what the speaker is saying. That is why when there is noise during speech delivery, the fastest means by which the speaker can control the noise is to start speaking again, at that the audience is forced to stop the noise so as to listen more. Inability to speak up also causes sleep when a speech is going on.

In most speeches, the loudness and lowness have a lot to say about the action involved. Some actions are better communicated forcefully-loud while others in a lower manner, this kind of variance also help to buttress the point better. Volume is the emphatic sign of italic or bold in a written text. Consequently, the secret of volume is discovered behind the scene and should be found before every delivery – practice, practice, practice.

Quality and Articulation:
Quality refers to how refined the voice of a speaker can be. For a speaker to increase the quality or the fluency of his voice in delivery, he should learn to: manipulate the mouth, tongue and breathing, speak free from any kind of obstruction in the mouth; and learn to slip and slide off the tongue from roof of the mouth and the back of the teeth, such observances will enable the speaker to adequately formulate the syllables needed to articulate words clearly. The speaker should make sure that nothing obstructs the free flow of the mouth when speaking whether internally or externally. Hence, the major problems of vocal quality centered on the excess nasality, breathiness, and huskiness and their faults in the use of vocal mechanism differ. The problems of vocal quality are surmountable only with serious practice.

A proper articulation in the speech is observed when the speech is distinct enough to e understood clearly. The slur or the mumble of words makes our speech meaningless and also bores every bit of the speech. The speaker should harden the muscle of the mouth in order to pronounce properly. A lazy pronunciation leads to a lazy speech. The speaker should discover the number of syllables in the words and where emphasis is to be placed when pronouncing a word. Example is pronouncing a word like: "practically" which is made up of four syllables: prac-ti-cal-ly. An incomplete pronunciation of the whole syllable of this word makes it very difficult for an audience to understand the meaning a speaker wants to communicate.

Cicero encourages orators to practice as much as possible even if they have failed once. He illustrates with the secret of Demosthenes the famous Athenian Orator, "let him press forward night and day (so to) in this single vocation, and do as the famous Athenian Demosthenes did, whose pre-eminence in oratory is unhesitatingly admitted, and whose zeal and exertions are said to have been such that at the very outset he surmounted natural drawbacks by diligent perseverance, and thought at first stuttering so badly as to be unable to pronounce the initial R of the name of the art of his devotion, by practice he made himself accounted as distinct a speaker as anyone; later on, though his breath was rather short, he succeeded so far in making his breath hold during a speech, that a single oratorical period – as his writings prove- covered two risings and two fallings of tone; moreover – as the tale goes – it was his habit to slip pebbles into his mouth, and then declaim a number of verses at the top of his voice and without drawing breath, and this not only as he stood still, but while walking about, or going up a steep slope. I think any orator who strives to improve often find himself at the top of the mount of victory."[112]

Pauses:

Pauses are temporal stops by a speaker. It is a time when the audience are given time to sink in the information they have gathered. It is often used, by speakers before or after a "compound word" (a word that embodies a lot of meanings) is used. It is also used when the speaker is still thinking about a suitable word or phrase to use in communicating a point better. Pauses in spoken words sometimes can serve as punctuation in the sentences being made and help to communicate the meanings effectively. Thus Duane buttresses this point when she said, "As you speak, you audience has no periods, commas semicolons, or dashed before them. They depend largely on your pauses to tell them what is to be distinguished from what. The pauses are not to be avoided or filled with "ers", "ums" or "ahs". They should be used to punctuate your speech; to separate clauses, phrases, and sentences from one another; to indicate stress or emphasis; to provide the natural rhythm so necessary to effective speech."[113]

Most naïve speakers are scared of pauses in a speech. They think it is a sign of weakness, and therefore they end up using an excessive nonverbal – fillers like: "ers", ums", or "ahs", and unarticulated phrases to ruin their speeches. Hence, a sufficient rehearsal by the speaker will always save him from such mistakes.

STAGE FRIGHT:

This is pertinent part most people will want to hear. Fear of public speaking is probably the most universal type of anxiety. It is a form of anticipatory anxiety.[114] Most speakers are frightened about meeting an audience, what can they offer to gain audience satisfaction? How can they win the audience's interest? What will be the fate of the day's delivery? These are the kinds of questions that always reflect in their hearts. Cicero remarks, "The better the orator, the more profoundly is the frightened of the difficulty of speaking, and of the doubtful fate of a speech, and of the anticipations of an audience."[115]

Some fright can be seen as part of the game, while others are destructive. Those that are part of the game are those that inform the body that things serious are going to take place. Example is the situation where the speaker notices an increase in the heart beating rate of breathing rate, or hand shaking and voice quavering. Thus Ferraro and Palmer opined, "Every speaker is nervous. But if your nervousness is apt to manifest itself in shaking hands, then grab hold to the sides of the podium. If your voice quavers, then speak a little more loudly and deeply. The signs of nervousness will go away after the first minute or two as the presentation of your argument takes control of your mind and body."[116]

The frights that are destructive are those that hinder the effectiveness of the delivery or that obstruct the delivery out rightly. "I once so utterly lost heart in opening an indictment, that I had to thank Quintus Maximums for doing me the Supreme service of promptly adjourning the hearing, the moment he saw that I was broken-down and unnerved by fear."[117] Cicero said. This kind of fright can manifest in the way of loss of memory, loss of reasoning, difficult in speech, instant headache or fever, Knees being wobbly etc.

To get rid of destructive stage fright always, practice unceasingly. Learn to prepare your speech and write it in the best way of appealing to the interest of the audience, then call a second observer to be around during your practices to assure you of a satisfied preparation. Try as much as you can to be comfortable with yourself mainly from your physical appearance: how you dress – Do not wear what you think you are not comfortable with; try to stand erect while you deliver your speech and stop bending on the lectern or grasping or clamping to things that are irrelevant unless you get much anxiety to settle; wear a smiling face at the start to enable you adapt to the audience. Such are the reinforcing smiles they will give you in return; disguise your nervousness till you observe the nervousness no more. As a general instruction, observe the words of Litfin, "first, you must work hard to develop a good speech, one which will be interesting, relevant, and informative, and one that you can look forward to delivering. And, send, you must so control the material of the speech that you are confident you will not forget it."[118] When these safety precautions have been taken care of by the speaker, the success level of the speaker can then move to a higher frequency.

CHAPTER NINE

HOW TO INTRODUCE YOUR SPEECH

In every speech, there must be a beginning no matter the type of speech and the personality of the person delivering the speech. This beginning goes a long way to determine the rest of your speech. Because of the relevance of this beginning to every speech, it is advised to always learn the modalities of introducing a speech in order to avoid poor deliverance.

A lot of people disgrace themselves when presenting a well prepared speech without a good beginning. Cicero out of his expertise encourages speakers on one of the modalities of introducing a speech when he says: "one's opening remarks though they should always be carefully framed and pointed and epigrammatic and suitably expressed, must at the same time be appropriate to the case in hand; for the opening passage contains the first impression and the introduction of the speech and this ought to charm and attract the hearer straight away."[119]

It is a fact that about 80 percent of an audience normally anticipates a goal and a gain, therefore, they will at the outset give the speaker their attention till they are disappointed. At the beginning of a speech, says Aristotle, "is just where is least slackness of interest; it is therefore ridiculous [to ask for your audience's attention] at the beginning, when everyone is listening with the most attention."[120] Just know that the ball is at your court and give the right kick. Do not begin your speech with cold words like: "my brother has said it all", "As my brother/sister rightly said before now". This makes the audience get bored of your speech even before they start to listen to you. Rather begin your speech as your own and not as another's speech.

A speaker betrays the trust and commitment of the audience by making a lousy beginning through the use of common words, clauses and sentences that may qualify as cliché, for instance: "it is a pleasure being here", "good morning ladies and gentlemen" and the likes. Be innovative; always discover new and more captivating ideas to gain your audience. Always bear in mind, "the first 30 seconds are the 'make or break' time for your presentation."[121]

The introductory part of a speech is not billed for long statements neither is it time to elaborate the main point of the whole write up in a way that bores the audience and seems to imply that their further listening is simply a waste of time. Precision matters a lot in the context of writing or delivering a speech. We should always learn and follow the right way. "Some speakers make certain they can distil the major objective of the speech into a 10-second statement. That one phrase captures the absolute essence of their theme and is included in the first two minutes of their speech."[122] An introduction structured in this way can do a magic of wetting the appetite of your audience.

The technicality of an introduction is one that demands caution. Our audience deserves to have an idea of the direction we are about to head, but not the means of getting there. This implies that, "in the introduction, you must fix the subject more precisely. You must state, or at least suggest, your proposition, and it is sometimes good to indicate how you intend to present your discussion."[123] One should be careful when scratching the main idea of the work at the introduction, lest we overstretch our boundary. We should also avoid beating about the bush or rigmarole with words like a ship without a rudder. Some find themselves talking so loud but outside purpose and content of the speech. Sherman advises, "Begin with the end in mind", start and finish by emphasizing the same major point."[124] The major point here is striking as a lead to the main aim of the speech.

Having taken cognizance of some of these nitty-gritty of introduction, there are few basic questions we should ask ourselves before setting out to write our introduction. We should at least know something about our audience and their interest on the issue you are about to treat. These questions might be helpful:[125]

1. Does the reader [audience] have any interest in my subject, or must I try to attract his attention?

2. If I have to attract his attention, how do I do it?

3. How ignorant is he of my subject? How much do I have to explain to give him a background for my discussion?

4. Am I merely trying to present something to him, or am I trying to convince him of something? If, in other words, he has a resistance to the view I am presenting, what attitude shall I take toward him?

These questions are necessary and should inform our pattern of introduction. It should also remind us of the central role of introduction to every speech, and while we must take it very seriously. A greater work is needed at the introduction. There is what is called an 'appetizer'- this is the nerve you strike in the audience in order to gain their attention keeping them in ecstasy or under spell. In order to strike this nerve as quick as possible, cram or memorize the first sentences or any relevant flashy part of your introduction. It must not be long but should be reasonable with no atom of inconsistency. Therefore, verbs used in an introduction should be transitive, thereby enkindling the fire of anticipation in the listeners.

However, in order not to fall into the impediment of wrong introduction. Litfin also outlines four major frameworks that can guide an introduction. They include:[126]

> Capturing the attention of the audience.
> Building rapport with the audience.
> Showing the audience why they should listen to the speech.
> Orienting the audience to the subject matter of the speech.

The act capturing the attention of the audience is a bit easy at the beginning but gets tougher when mishandled. A speaker should bear in mind the uniqueness of his audience, the varieties of their sentiments, and their unequal levels of understanding in order to avoid missing their attention at the start of his speech. So therefore, one should try as much as possible to know what the audience needs to hear at any given moment in order to satisfy their desire. This is because human beings do not babble with reasoning alone, their feelings are also part of the processes of language and understanding. As Warren would have it, "A human being isn't merely a machine for logical thought. Thought shades off into feeling, and feeling shades off into thought. We cannot exclude feeling from our experience, nor should we wish to do so, but we do want our life of feeling and our life of thought to be consistent with each other, to make some kind of total sense."[127] For a speaker to guide his audience through this right process of human language without allowing either feeling or reason to suppress the other, every speaker should be familiar with some of these major devices for moving an audience.

MAJOR DEVICES FOR WINNING AN AUDIENCE

There are many devices that can enable the speaker gain the consciousness of his audience. The major among these are briefly highlighted below. Good management or application of these devices can make a difference.

a) Humor: People want to hear some humorous incidents, jokes and witty remarks. Nobody wants to look at a face that looks like a foe. They want to see joy radiate in the face of a speaker so as to enkindle their own excitement. Fulton once observes that, 'a touch of humor at the beginning is a good approach and the best humor is that which is directed against self."[128] Device a good humor today if you are determined to hold your audience spell bound till the end of your speech.

b) Emotion: Most people are emotional and sentimental in nature that a little play on their emotion makes them loose control of themselves. They want to hear events or stories that are emotional: sympathetic, sorrowful, lovely etc. Adolf Hitler, once remarked: Only a storm of hot passion can turn the destinies of people, and he alone can arouse passion who bears it within himself. It alone gives its chosen one the words which like hammer blows can open the gates to the heart of a people. But the man whom passion fails and whose lips are sealed – has not been chosen by Heaven to proclaim its will.[129] Engage the audience in a hot emotion and it will sustain them till the end of your speech.

c) Novelty:

They want to hear about the latest discovery in science; forecast, prophecy or prediction, an idea which they don't know already etc. Apart from this, they also want to hear what is reasonable and logical whether true or false, for 'one of the wonders of oratory is that even false predictions, can still move the audience!'

d) Oddity:

People want to hear unusual, abnormal, extraordinary, strange and other things that are far from their sphere of anticipation. They easily get bored of redundant stories; they need a story that can move them to greater imagination and wonder.

e) Conflict:

They want to hear about a place where horrible things are happening anywhere in the world, but more especially around. They want to hear about War, genocide, Xenophobia, ethnic cleansing, riot, fighting or any other related issues of disagreement and "cognitive inconsistency".

f) Sex:
People want to hear of stories relating to gender, rapes, sexual aberrations and other "sex elements". Once people hear about such stories, they want to know where they happened. They want to share their sympathy with those involved, they want to know the reaction of law enforcement agents towards such crime. They also want to know the gender, age and race of the victim. Such stories provide for the audience good food for thought.

g) Intensity:
The audiences are enthused when they hear the speaker paint a distinct picture of events. Their attention is also stolen from them by the speaker in the use of particularity, colorful or flashy wordings delivered with strength. An example is a forceful quotation, proverb, or idioms.

h) Coherency:
People want to hear logically valid arguments; word or sentences that have an adequate chain of connections. This implies that in every speech, "the elements of the discourse must stick together. This may seem to be simply another way of saying that a discourse must have unity. Unity and coherence are, indeed related.... In unity, the emphasis is on the relation of the various elements of a discourse to the dominant topic. In coherence, the emphasis is on the order – the continuity – of

the elements."[130] When a speaker losses consistency in speech or unity, he invariably losses his audience.

i) Familiarity:

This involves comments that are closer to the people's sphere of existence, and easy for people to have immediate knowledge as it is being communicated. People want to be noticed, they want to assure themselves that their being is not lost and so are happy to hear the speaker say what they have heard before. This can boast their ego. It can be a popular proverb, an epigram, quotations, etc.

j) Proximity:

People are more apt to listen to stories that relate to them or to their locality or country. That is why many people are ethnocentric in their actions. Hence, the best way to begin your speech is to begin with the latest news in the national dailies or things that happened around your vicinity.

k) Progress:

People want to hear about successful news, the latest development in science, the latest car, house, book. All these are dependent on the caliber of audience present. Nobody wants to hear stories of failure which might lead them into anxiety *(angst)* or despair. Your audience loves to hear you speak with heavy optimism rather than hearing you being pessimistic.

l) Suspense:
Challenging rhetorical questions, half baked interesting stories, strange gesture and so on, can keep the interest of the audience lively from the start till the end of any speech. Try as much as you can to clarify whatever you might have used to keep the audience in suspense before the end of the speech.

J) Religion:
Religion has a great force of drawing people's interest, especially when it is ones religion, or a rival religion. So many people want to hear about the progress of their religion, and how it has contributed positively or miraculously to people's life. They also want to hear how their rival religions or denominations false and wouldn't lead to salvation. They simply want the flops of other religions to be discussed and they are ready to listen to that whenever.

k) Economy:
In a world that is beseeched with global economic crisis, and many economic imbalances. So many people want to hear about the state of the world or their national economy and how it affects their daily life. They want to know the state of the economy in the years to come. They already have basic ideas, and when you key in with facts, they simply listens.

L) Health:
In an age beseeched by many diseases most of which have defied the high technological breakthrough in sciences. Everybody is out to know the right steps to a healthy life and body fitness. Almost everybody is involved in this category because health they say is wealth. Information about new sickness, technological advancement in the area of drug discoveries, and personal health awareness captures a lot of attention.

M) Self-Interest:
Human nature structures us to think and judge from our own perspective. We want to see life from our own spectacle, and we simply pick interest whenever anything concerning us is being discussed. Even the most boring audience would listen up whenever any matter about them is being discussed.

These devices are to be handled professionally and with serious precautions. They are to be applied without excessive sensationalism, gimmickry, use of weak questions which deserve no reactions, unnecessary elongated stories. The result is always an unbroken, high degree of attention from an audience.

EXAMPLES OF AN INTRODUCTORY SPEECH:

"Experience' they say, "is the best teacher". That is the main purpose of presenting here a sample of those papers presented in the past by great orators of our time and in history. These examples may not be the best in history; rather your own paper which should be the product of your experience might be the best paper.

EXAMPLE ONE:[131]
The speech delivered on 21 September 1953 by Nelson Rohihlala Mandela, the first black president of South Africa, elected in 1994. A renowned lawyer and politician, he led the South Africans to a non-racist democracy. He delivered this speech before his 27 years imprisonment from 1960. Here is introduction of Mandela's speech:

Since 1912 and year after year thereafter, in their homes and local areas, in provincial and national gathering on trains and buses, in the factories and on the farms, in cities, villages, discussed the shameful misdeeds of those who rule the country. Year after year, they have raised their voices in condemnation of grinding poverty of the people, the low wages, the acute shortage of land, the inhuman exploitation and the whole policy of white domination. But instead of more freedom, repression began to grow in volume and intensity, and it seemed that all their sacrifices would end up in smoke and dust. Today the entire country knows that their labours were not in vain for a new spirit, and new ideas have gripped our people. Today the people speak the language of action. There is a mighty awakening among the men and women of our country and the year 1952 stands out as the year of this upsurge of national consciousness.

EXAMPLE TWO:
The much anticipated-speech before a joint session of Congress delivered on 20 September 2001 by President George W. Bush. The speech was in response to the tragic incident of 11 September 2001 when four large jets were hijacked and piloted into the twin towers of the World Trade Centre at New York and the Pentagon at Washington, killing over 3,000 persons. Here is the introductory part of Bush's speech:

Mr Speaker, Mr President Pro Tempore, members of Congress, and fellow Americans:

In the normal course of events, presidents come to this chamber to report on the state of the Union. Tonight, no such report is needed. It has already been delivered by the American people.

We have seen it in the courage of passengers who rushed terrorists to save others on the ground. Passengers like an exceptional man named Todd Beamer. And would you please help me welcome his wife Lisa Beamer here tonight?

We have seen the state of our Union in the endurance of rescuers working past exhaustion.

We've seen the unfurling of flags, the lightening of candles, the giving of blood, the saying of prayers in English, Hebrew and Arabic.

We have seen the decency of a loving and giving people who have made the grief of strangers their own.

My fellow citizens, for the last nine days, the entire world has seen for itself the state of the Union, and it is strong.

Tonight, we are a country awakened to danger and called to defend freedom. Our grief has turned to anger to resolution. Whether we bring our enemies to justice or bring justice to our enemies, justice will be done.

I thank the Congress for its leadership at such an important time.

EXAMPLE THREE:
A speech delivered at the Labour Party national conference in August 2005, by Anthony Charles Lyndon Blair the prime minister of United Kingdom, First Lord of the Treasury, and Minister for the Civil Service. The speech was prompted by the London Bombing. Here is the introductory part of Blair's speech:

The greatest danger is that we fail to face up to the nature of the threat we are dealing with. What we witnessed in London last Thursday week was not an aberrant act. It was not random. It was not a product of particular local circumstance in West Yorkshire.

Senseless though any such horrible murder is, it was not without sense for its organizers. It had a purpose. It was done according to a plan it was meant. What we are confronting here is an evil ideology. It is not a clash of civilizations – all civilized people Muslim or others feel revulsion at it. But it is a global struggle and it is a battle of ideas, hearts and minds, both within Islam and outside it. This is the battle that must be won, a battle not just about the terrorist methods but their views. Not just their barbaric acts, but their barbaric ideas. Not only what they do but what they think and the thinking they would impose on others.

This ideology and the violence that is inherent in it did not start a few years ago in response to a particular policy. Over the past 12 years, al-Qaeda and its associates have attacked 26 countries, killed thousands of people, many of them Muslims. They have networks in virtually every country and thousands of fellow travellers. They are well-financed. Look at their websites. They aren't unsophisticated in their propaganda. They recruit however and whoever they can and with success. Neither is it true they have no demands. They do. It is just that no sane person would negotiate on them.

This is a religious ideology.... Those who kill in its name believe genuinely that in doing it, they do God's work; they go to paradise. They demand the elimination of Israel; the withdrawal of all Westerners Muslim countries, irrespectively Taliban states and Sharia law in the Arab world en route to one caliphate of all Muslim nations.

We don't have to wonder what type of country those states would be. Afghanistan was such a state. Girls put out of school. Women denied even rudimentary rights. People living in abject poverty and oppression. All of it justified by reference to religious faith.

EXAMPLE FOUR:

The speech delivered on 4 June 2009, by Barrack Obama, the first African-American president of America, elected in 2008. A renowned lawyer and Orator. He delivered this speech in Cairo, Egypt in one of the peace talk and dialogue with

Muslims. The speech was titled "A New Beginning." Here is the introduction of Obama's speech:

I am honoured to be in the timeless city of Cairo, and to be hosted by two remarkable institutions. For over a thousand years, Al-Azhar has stood as a beacon of Islamic learning, and for over a century, Cairo University has been a source of Egypt's advancement. Together, you represent the harmony between tradition and progress. I am grateful for your hospitality, and the hospitality of the people of Egypt. I am also proud to carry with me the goodwill of the American people, and a greeting of peace from Muslim communities in my country: assalaamu alaykum.

We meet at a time of tension between the United State and Muslims around the world – tension rooted in historical forces that go beyond current policy debate. The relationship between Islam and the West includes centuries of co-existence and cooperation, but also conflict and religious wars. More recently, tension has been fed by colonialism that denied rights and opportunities to many Muslims, and a Cold War in which Muslim-majority countries were too often treated as proxies without regard to their own aspirations. Moreover, the sweeping change brought by modernity and globalization led many Muslims to view the West as hostile to the traditions of Islam.

Violent extremists have exploited these tensions in a small but potent minority of Muslims. The attacks of September 11th, 2001 and the continued efforts of these extremists to engage in violence against civilians has led some in my country view Islam as inevitably hostile not only to America and Western counties, but also to human rights. This has bred more fear and mistrust.

So long as our relationship is defined by our differences, we will empower those who sow hatred rather than peace, and who promote conflict rather than the cooperation that can help all of our people achieve justice and prosperity. This cycle of suspicion and discord must end.

I have come here to seek a new beginning between the United States and Muslims around the world; one based upon mutual interest and mutual respect; and one based upon the truth that America and Islam are not exclusive, and need not be in competition. Instead, they overlap, and share common principles – principles of justice and progress; tolerance dignity of all human beings.

CHAPTER TEN

HOW TO UNDERSTAND YOUR AUDIENCE

The audience is the number one target of every good speaker. The absence of either passive or active audience is equal to the absence of speech. This is the more reason why every speaker should be conversant with the behavior or psychological makeup of his audience in order to be able to know how to address them and keep up their interest.

However, audience varies and so do speakers. A lot of factors govern the behavior and the relationship of audience, and we are going to look into these factors. The ability of a speaker to go into profound analysis or studies of the audience, and how environment, gender, etc. can affect a speech makes the particular speaker a genius. The necessary factors that affect the audience/speaker relationships are classified into the external and internal factors.

EXTERNAL FACTORS
A lot of external and concrete factors reasonably affect the speeches we make. These factors are quite negligible, and they include:

The Population of the Audience:
So many speakers fidget at the sight of a larger audience. This might be as a result of the diversities in the thought of such an audience of the personalities that make up such audience. It can also be as a result that larger audiences are

more prone to distractions than when they are fewer. In line with this, Litfin added that, larger numbers of audience inevitably bring greater diversity, and the more diverse the audience, the more difficult it is to focus clearly upon the common needs of the audience. Indeed, in a large audience one often discovers several sub-audiences with distinct differences. When this diversity is combined with the increased anxiety many speakers experience when they face a sizable group of people, it is not difficult to see why many speakers try to avoid large groups.[132]

Consequently, a lot of people have no personal opinion when they find themselves in the midst of a group or more still, a lot of people believe that a single person cannot win the majority in the tribunal of simple argument. Hence, popular saying goes that, 'if you can't beat them, then you join them'. Among the advantages of a highly populated audience is that there is no such room for dialogue, which can lead to a victor or vanquish position between the audience and speakers. Once a greater majority of an audience accepts a proposition, others inevitably join.

Furthermore, the co-cordiality, the extreme closeness or more person to person relationship is minimal in a populated audience. Speakers are saved from extreme questioning and weighing of their opinion. Also the distance from the speaker to the audience is increased thereby giving a speaker more control over his audience.

Situation:

The situation a speaker finds himself goes a long way to determine the precaution a speaker should take. Some occasions are formal while others are informal. The ability of a speaker to adapt to the situation he finds himself makes him a good speaker. Formal speeches demand serious preparation and follow a strict method of speech presentation.

On the other hand, informal speeches can be presented with any methodology in so far as the ethics of communication is never neglected. A speaker who is conscious of variation in speeches usually makes a great difference in the life of his audience.

Environment:
Environment has a lot of impact on the audience; it determines the capacity of assimilation and dissimilation of speeches. Good and organized of assimilation and dissimilation of speeches. Good and organized environment contribute in a good speech presentation and good understanding.

The design of the venue of the speech presentation matters a lot. 'As a general rule, your goal should be to schedule your speeches in stings your audience will find as pleasant as possible."[133]

Consequently, the hall and the internal settings of the venue of speech presentation – seat, space, ventilation, light and sounds should be designed to enhance the comfort of the audience. There should be enough seats to accommodate the audience. The arrangement of the hall should be in such a way that the audience do not just scatter themselves in a big hall; rather they should sit closer and nearer to the speaker to enhance more effective communication. The audience has also the right to enjoy fresh air and a normal temperature.

The microphone also should not be a distraction to the people it should be set moderately. More still, the role of light cannot be neglected, people are scared by darkness and they don't feel comfortable being in the dark.

Conclusively, proper attention should be given to the audience's welfare so as to create a balanced situation for both the speaker and the audience in order to ensure effective communication.

INTERNALFACTORS:
There are those complex intrinsic factors, which though important are not perceptible to our physical eyes. These factors are more useful to a speaker depending on the audience composition – whether homogeneous or heterogeneous. Heterogeneous audiences are more difficult to handle than homogeneous ones. The speaker of a heterogeneous audience tries to touch a lot of things or a lot of ways people view things, so as to avoid hurting the sentiments of the audience.

A lot of factors lead to the variation in the homogeneity and heterogeneity of an audience, but this work shall concentrate on the major ones:

Sex:
Sex most often irrelevant, but in some cases, they need not to be neglected. A topic like 'how to learn a car' does not demand the sex make up of the audience before you can give your speech. But a topic like, 'who are the victims of rape', is very sensitive and demands good knowledge of the sex make up of your audience population.

In a situation of mixed audience, Liftin will admonish that, "in dealing with material that is affected by sex differences, the best course of action may be to think in terms of two "audience" and attempt to adapt to the needs of both throughout the speech."[134]

Cultural and Ethnic Background:
Culture they say is the "life of the people", "it is a mode of living proper to a society"[135] therefore, every society or ethnic background have a way of living associated with it. Culture varies; a lot of things which are valid in a particular culture might be invalid in another. Let the speaker respect cultural difference, and not assume that he can do anything anywhere and get away with it. Learn the culture of the people you are going to address and be a good carrier of culture, by then, you would have succeeded in helping your audience realize their being. According to Mondin, "man is not natural, but a cultural being: this means that at the moment of birth, nature gave hardly the necessary minimum, the essentials, to be man, and assigns him the task of making himself and forming himself so as to fully realize his being through culture."[136]

Social Status:
There are three major social statuses – the upper, middle or lower classes. But the most predominant are the upper and lower classes as in the days of Karl Marx. The lower class people most often tend to have low self esteem, and need just reinforcement and encouragement. While the upper class needs prestige and praise, they have passed some relevant levels in life. Being at the physiology level of Abraham Maslow's hierarchy of needs, they now think of some other heights to achieve.

More so, there is a big difference between the mentalities of people in the developing or under-developing countries. However, the speaker should try in every mixed class audience never to neglect a group or to hurt any groups' sentiments.

Educational Level and Intelligence:
In this aspect, the maxim that 'presumption is a vice' holds true. The speaker should not overgeneralize anything because that may be dangerous. Do not assume that because the audience is not a cream of medical doctors; therefore they have no knowledge of medicine. It is good to understand that some people even though their area of specialization is not on medicine, might still have passed through a medical class.

Consequently, never take your audience for granted. Be very much sensitive so as to know the educational levels of your audience may be through questioning or interviews. If you are talking either below or above the level of your audience, they are apt to lose attention. The rule is, learn the virtue of middle with extreme sensitivity and when to apply it.

Attitudes and Beliefs of the Audience:
Every culture has sets of attitudes and beliefs that influence nearly all aspects of human behavior and help to bring order to that society and its individuals.[137] A belief is the feeling that something is real and true; a trust; confidence, conviction, faith etc. Examples are: 'Christianity is a true religion,' and 'Obi is a boy'. While attitude, is a way of feeling, thinking or behaving. It is also a reflection of positive or negative feelings about a belief or some other object of attention.

Belief and attitude can be either positive or negative. The picture is further complicated by the fact that beliefs and attitudes exist in widely varying strengths, from strongly positive to strongly negative.

The evidence seems to suggest that people's view when stated publicly tends to be stronger and more resistant to change than views which have been kept private; views which have been acted upon will be stronger still. What is more in any given situation is that a person's attitude may temporarily conflict with another person's attitude. In any case, it is not difficult to see that an auditor's belief system will influence how he or she perceives both speaker and speech.[138] The ability of a speaker to accommodate the belief system of his audience in his speech helps him to harness all the attention of his audience.

Attitude toward Time:
People of different cultures have different conceptions of time and that is what guides their response to time schedule. Thus, Uzomah writes, "time is important in the United States, and much emphasis is placed on it." He further writes the remark on the explanation on the concept of time by an American who has worked in the Middle East for 20 years, he wrote: "A lot of the misunderstanding between Middle Easterners and Foreigners are due to their different concepts of time and space. At worst, there is no concept at all of time in the Middle East. At best, there is a sort of open-ended concept."[139] Most people in Africa are not time conscious either and so it is in many parts of the world. A good understanding of people's attitude to time will help the speaker to know what to expect from the particular audience about punctuality and duration of speech.

Attitude to Foreigners:
Africa is popularly known as a 'home of hospitality'. They have regards for strangers and can sacrifice their comfort, for the sake of a stranger, but in the case of Europe and America, they have an individualistic pattern of life which makes them maintain a loose relationship with foreigners of low statues more than those of high status.

TEMPERAMENTAL DISPOSITIONS:

Our dispositions in nature affect our ways of thinking, feeling and behaving. The human natural endowments, biological inheritance or temperaments have indeterminable and indefinite possibilities, and as such have enormous influence in human character formation. Temperament constitutes that part of human personality that made up of emotional dispositions and reactions, in their speed and intensity. It is a term normally used to refer to the enduring mood or mood pattern of a person.[140]

Hippocrates, the Greek philosopher and father of medicine, discovered four different personalities or temperaments that can differentiate individual characters. Individuals are made up of four different fluids (humors) which guide their characters. The sanguine he said have a lot of blood, the melancholic he identified as having a black bile, the cholerics are made up of yellow bile while the phlegmatic phlegm. The consciousness and adequate knowledge of individual differences will enable the speaker assess his audience at any time and to know their disposition and the right way to address them at any given time. Here are more detailed explanations of human temperaments:

The Sanguine:
The Sanguine are happy and carefree people who enjoy free association with others. They are sympathetic, sensitive people. They are emotionally weak and this makes them respond blindly to stimuli. They are so much scared at stressful moments. The sanguine tries their best to resist stress by trying to forget their problem by many ways like, over eating and drinking their dispositions to shade out extreme mental disturbances makes them forget a lot; forget appointments, and some daily activities. They are sentimental and emotional and will make a good audience for speakers who apply a little dose of humor to their speeches. The

sentimentality of the sanguine can also favor speakers with good or interesting stories. Avoid being too logical in dealing with the sanguine, avoid allowing longer quiet moments. Try to be cheerful and friendly.

Choleric:
They are ever committed to duty and abhor idleness. They are courageous, determined, and are good in arguments. They are ideologists with greater insight and higher sense of value. Their qualities make them leaders wherever they are. They sometimes find it difficult to keep friends because they have little time for themselves and for others.

Choleric don't like those who are not measuring up with them and they therefore find it difficult to accommodate such people. They are prone to stress but they can also manage stress because of their high rate of egotism. They like statements that go straight to the point and are therefore not too emotional. They have little or no time for pleasure.

A good speaker conscious of a choleric audience should try as much as possible to avoid long statements, illogicality and hasty conclusions. The speaker should also avoid dull speeches and should try to appeal to the reason of his audience and never their sentiments choleric audience good audience.

Melancholies:
They are mainly perfectionists who want to do everything well without mistakes. They have foresight, which is sometimes affected by their indecisiveness, lack of courage and so on. They are fault finders in others and difficult to please. They find it difficult to associate with people more

successful than they because it makes them feel inferior. They often bear grudges and are jealous. They sometimes wear dull looks, and it is difficult to discern whether they are happy or not. They are highly sensitive and are always frightened about failure.

A speaker addressing such group of people should avoid using harsh words or statements. He should avoid stressing them often with questions, he should not discern their inward feelings from externals, and he should try to be friendly as much as possible. Know it well that melancholic audiences are difficult to please and are prone to internal or under-desk critics.

Phlegmatic:
Phlegmatic(s) are easy going in nature. They ponder their problems alone within their heart. They don't care about what others are doing; they therefore, build a private world for themselves within. They are humble and quiet, good listeners, friendly, sympathetic, and creative. They are self-centered and this makes it difficult for people to go with them because, they don't understand the feelings of others – they are indifferent to other people's feelings. They are lazy in appearance, indecisive and most often feel superior to others. They are witty and sometimes humorous. They have a pessimistic view of things, behave fearfully and sometimes unemotionally.

A good speaker addressing the phlegmatic(s) should know that, they are witty in nature. They try to hide their feelings always. It is difficult to arouse their emotions or to make them free their minds and this makes them difficult to be convinced. The ability to convince them wins them on the speaker's side.

Consequently, temperaments are difficult to be identified and require a lot of observations and in-depth studies. Nobody has a single temperament but will always have a domineering temperament. In a group, it is difficult to get a common temperament but once a speaker notices the greatest or the domineering temperament in the group, he can make a difference in the life of his audience.

Furthermore, communication starts once two people come together to talk or sign in order to pass information. So in a minimal populace, the greater use of temperament can make the greatest impact ever recorded. Take time to study your audience, and know that early arrival and a silent observation of the audience will make them open up their real temperaments.

DISTINCTIVENESS OF AUDIENCE ACCORDING TO AGE:

This behavior and the cognitive development of human beings vary depending on age difference. And so do the needs interest and motivation of man vary on age bases. Since there is a lot of variance at different ages, the speaker should make sure he never leaves out any age group. He should therefore try to balance his speeches so as not to favor a particular age group more than the other. The adult are bored at kid stories and children are bored of adult stories, therefore, a greater task faces a speaker of a mixed age audience in balancing such speeches to the admiration of all present.

The reactions and the level of understanding by the audience are determined by the level of the audience. Children see things differently from adolescents and so do adults.

Speakers should be sensitive enough to know their audience and relate with them in relation to their age levels.

SOCIAL PERCEPTION OF PEOPLE:

Every individual is guided by two major social processes which include: the process of forming impressions of people, and the process of attributing causes to people's behavior.

IMPRESSION FORMATION:
Different impressions are created once people come in contact with others. Among the catalysts of these impressions are physical characteristics such as the person's sex skin color, height, dressing etc. when people see these characteristics, they tend to make a lot of associations and interpretations. We often find ourselves drawing inferences and generalization of what we think a particular thing is on the inside.

The verbal and nonverbal aspects of a person also contribute in the creation of impressions. Fluent people control more attention more than quiet ones. And so do body languages have a lot to say about a person.

Impression formation is a search to discover how the audience creates a portrait of the speaker and how the speaker constructs his portrait in return. These generalizations about others are often guided by people's first impressions and social scheme.

First Impressions:
This is the first assumption we make once we see a person for the first time. This initial impression lasts more than the latter impression because human beings like novelty and

once they see a person for the first time, they are more attentive and this makes the first information gathered to be clearly remembered.

"First impression provides a framework or central theme around which all subsequent information is organized. Information that is consistent with the first impression will be integrated with it; whole discrepant information that does not fit well with our initial view may be distorted or even disregarded."[141] A good speaker should try as much as possible to be active and vibrant at first speech presentation, in order to create an enduring positive impression. Good impression enables a speaker to create a good rapport with his audience.

Social Schemas:
Zimbardo sees schemas as the categories and organizing principles that we use to make sense of the world around us.[142] Audiences are usually of the habit of using schemas to interpret information about a speaker. Social schemas can be subdivided into: implicit personality theory, prototype and stereotypes.

Implicit Personality Theory:
This involves certain expectations about how traits fit together and the use of these expectations both to evaluate others and to infer characteristics and traits that have not actually been noticed.

Audiences are sometimes moved to perceive speakers in the light of implicit personality theory. They believe that certain personality traits are related to each other. Example, if we have the conception that French people are proud, whenever we see a French person or speaker, we hastily conclude that,

that person will be proud – even if we have not observed that particular French person to know if he is proud or not.

Prototype: It is the standard or supposed "typical example" against which we match the person we are evaluating.[143] We tend most often to associate a particular personality with a set of traits. Example, a prototype of a homosexual might include such traits like shyness. Generous, femininity, et cetera.

Speakers are advised to know the kind of character they display before their audience lest they will be misinterpreted by their audience.

Stereotypes: This is a characteristic that is usually associated with a particular group. Once a person introduces himself as a lawyer, it is assumed that lawyers are intelligent, principled, and serious etc., therefore, this lawyer in particular is intelligent, principled, and serious.

Moreover, stereotypes have either or both positively or negatively valued characteristics. The term "stereotype" often has a negative connotation in popular usage because it refers to biased, over- simplified views about another ethnic, racial, or religious group, which are used as basis for the rejection of its members. As such, stereotypes are often seen as central cognitive mechanism in the development and maintenance of prejudice.[144]

Impression in Status Transactions:
Status transactions refer to "forms of communication between people that establish their relative statuses, their social power, and their territorial control. These transactions often involve moment-by moment adjustments of each person's status."[145]

A good speaker should create a high status impression about himself in order to be able to enhance satisfaction in his audience. High status can be achieved when a speaker carries himself and duty with dignity, responsibility and authority by:

- Maintaining a very good posture that is erect and stable.
- Moment should be gentle and purposeful.
- The movement of the components of the body should be intact and mechanical.
- Making a good and articulated speech with an average speaking rate.
- Making a good eye contact with your audience.
- Standing firmly while speaking.
- Maintaining a good posture while sitting.

The status transaction moderates the judgment on audience about a speaker and this will either enable the speaker control attention or make him lose it. Naturally, high status people control much attention than lower status people.

MAKING YOUR AUDIENCE FRIENDS:
A good speaker has to be a good friend to his audience. This is because people like to listen to their friends more than any other person. This friendship is not just created, a lot of things foster it. People are generally united by their common

belief, objective, behaviors and values, but there are other major factor that could also foster friendship. These include:

Similarity:
The audience most often, appreciates people that resemble them in anyway. This makes them feel that people like them are capable of doing a lot of things. It increases their self-esteem and makes them comfortable to listen more to the speaker.

Complementarity:
Audiences appreciate persons who are an opposite of them in order to enable them acquire what they don't have already; namely, new things and ideas.

Reciprocity:
When a speaker, through words and actions, shows his audience that he loves or appreciate them, the audience is often consciously or unconsciously moved top pay back the love in return through listening attentively.

Physically Attractiveness:
Those who have very good body build-up tend to control great attention. People admire beautiful persons, because they most often associate beauty with goodness, friendliness, brilliance, and so on. That is why a speaker should practice good postures and also take adequate care of himself so as to be attractive.

Proximity:
People like those who come nearer to them and share with them. The humility of the speaker therefore matters. Speakers are advised to be as close as possible to their audience in order to establish the necessary close relationship.

QUALITIES OF FRIENDSHIP:

There are many qualities which people admire in friends, and once they observe such qualities in a person, they are much more attracted to the person. Such qualities may include:

Supportiveness:
People admire those who proffer solutions to other people's problems. They need a helping hand, and people who can always reason with them in order to improve their conditions.

Intelligence:
This is a rare characteristic found in people. Very few are gifted with the gift of intelligence and majority of them rarely develop theirs. So, once people see an intelligent person, they tend to submit their will and attentions in order to improve themselves.

Sincerity:
Nobody wants to associate with a liar, and nobody wants to be deceived either. Once people or an audience observes the truthfulness in the point the speaker is making, they tend to give an undivided attention, therefore building a good rapport with the speaker.

Sense of humor:
In the modern world where there is high increase in human level of anxiety; people see any source of happiness as a means of curing these anxieties. They therefore, like to associate with people with great sense of humor in order to entertain themselves with that happiness they desire. A good speaker gains the attention of his audience, and also makes his audience friends with proper application of humor.

Affection:
People like those who show gestures of love or kindly feelings towards them. They love to be treated mildly, and they enjoy being petted so much. Good speakers should in words and actions display affection to their audience so as to gain their friendship.

Willing to Make out Time for Others:
People enjoy those who sacrifice their time for their sake, and they feel that such a person loves them so much. A speaker can manifest this by creating out time to explain a particular thing gradually to the understanding of even the least person of his audience. They see such a speaker as one who cares.

Good Conversationalist:
A speaker who has nothing to convey to his audience makes his audience foes. This is because the audience may have forfeited a lot of programs for the day, in order to come and listen and gain the satisfaction they need. So when they find a speaker quibbling, they feel insulted.

THE PSYCHOLOGY OF THE AUDIENCE:
Psychology helps to study the behavior and mental processes of human beings, the way they behave, why they behave that way, and so on. Hence, humanistic psychologists view human beings as organisms that have built-in social needs; and so require interpersonal relationships to become what they are capable of being.

Abraham H. Maslow, a former professor in Brooklyn College, a Chairman of the department of psychology at Brandeis University, and a humanistic psychologist whose studies on human motivation have helped us in formulating the basic general psychological assumptions about the members of our audience. Maslow articulated a lot of motives that govern human behavior. Ezechukwu highlights that, "for Maslow, when people are motivated not so much by unmet needs as by the desire to become all they are capable of, then they are seeking self-actualization. This means, for example, exploring and enhancing relationships with others, following interest for pure pleasure rather than for status or esteem, and being concerned with issues affecting all people, not just oneself."[146]

However, Maslow continues by elucidating that the highest motivation is that of self actualization which is only attained by a few. The ability to attain this greatest hierarchy of needs is dependent upon the people's goals: some people have a low level of goal that they long for the high goals. Other reasons why some don't reach the highest goal are because of environmental factors – man is a product of his environment.

Consequently, Maslow characterizes these motivational needs in a pyramidal order so as to represent the hierarchical and developmental way, in order of strength and of priority."[147] The need for representing these needs as a pyramid is to visually show that not everybody can reach the apex or Zenith of the pyramid since it is sloppy. Some can end their effort and strength. The five levels of the classification of needs in Maslow include:

- Physiological needs
- Safety needs
- Love needs

- Esteem needs
- The need for self actualization.

Fig. 10. 1: Below is the representation of Maslow's hierarchy of needs in a pyramid:

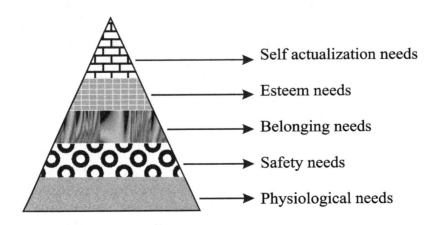

PHYSIOLOGICAL NEEDS:
This need is found at the base of Maslow's pyramid, it is the most primitive need. It involves the satisfaction of the fundamental needs like hunger, thirst, sensory stimulation, maintaining a body temperature, and "even the gratification of sex."[148] At a relaxation gallery where philosophy was normally discussed were inscribed: "Those who have not satisfied their basic necessities of life should not come to the agora". This level of needs is a major problem of the under-developing countries and a minor one in the developed countries. It is said that, "a hungry man is an angry man". So audiences who have not crossed the physiological stage of life find it difficult to listen to a speech which is academically oriented.

SAFETY NEEDS:
This need involves an innate proneness in human beings to seek for protection or security. The child would like to be protected from danger, threat, fear, he needs to enjoy the serenity of body and soul in a world free danger and fears. The adult also in the bid to protect himself move for documented contracts, insurances, social security, the protection of law and forces in order to gain security. The first level of need must be satisfied before this level. However, Maslow maintained that, these safety needs must be gratified. It can't be pushed ahead because the ungratified safety needs will remain forever underground, always calling for satisfaction.[149]

Assuring safety for audience who belongs to this particular hierarchy will do. They also need a lot of proofs before they can entrust their confidence in the orator. They also need to be encouraged to move ahead and never lose heart.

LOVE AND BELONGING NEEDS:
This is level of association and affection; people at this level try to belong to various primary groups, such as family, and to secondary group, such as club, ethnic group, or nationality.[150] The individual also break away from any type of isolation and launch into seeking other's affection; especially of opposite sex. These relationships sometimes have sexual components but the main desire for sex comes under physiological needs.

ESTEEM NEEDS:
This is a need to be appreciated by others in the society, the need for value and self-worth. In order to stratify this need, the individual tries to show his competence, confidence and

achievement in order that these be appreciated. When people appreciate all these efforts, the person increases in self esteem, and vice versa.

The speaker should know that audiences at this level are usually boastful and arrogant. They need good complements as a sort of re-enforcement, anything contrary to this, can turn off their spirits.

SELF-ACTUALIZATION NEEDS:
This is the highest level of needs attained by a few. It is the most complex of all because of the difficulty in attaining to such heights. It can also be seen as a final refinement of goals in life, because at this stage, one who studies engineering is now an engineer. Maslow observed that, achieving basic need gratification gives us many peak experiences, each of which are absolute delights, perfect in themselves, and needing no more than themselves to validate life.[151]

Hence, if self-actualization needs seem dormant in most people at most times, it is because the list of needs we just examined constitutes a hierarchy and the self-actualization needs come to the fore only as the other needs are being reasonably satisfied. Obviously, if a person is dying of thirst or is sitting in the midst of an artillery bombardment, the need for safety takes priority. In these situations, belonging, esteem, and self-actualization needs are quite put beside.

Likewise, fulfilling the need for a sense of belonging takes precedence over esteem and self-actualization and becomes almost a precondition or means of meeting those higher needs. It is only when our physical and safety needs are satisfied and we have come to a reasonable sense of belonging and self-worth that the matter of self-actualization becomes a motivating force in our lives.[152]

From the foregoing, it is clear that the audiences have an unavoidable part to play in every speech presentation. Without the audience, there will not be anything like speech presentation, and as shown above, their behavior, psychology, attitude and natural reactions especially during speech presentation matter enormously.

The Art of Oratory

CHAPTER ELEVEN

HOW TO EFFECTIVELY PERSUADE AN AUDIENCE

In our free and sentimental society, there is a greater inclination to persuasive speeches than other forms. Politicians, media, scientists, philosophers, economists, *et cetera* all tend in one way or the other to persuade us to reason in their line of thought.

Persuasion can be defined as the act of influencing others with whatever course you aim at making them accept. It can also be defined as "the use of the various resources of discourse to influence the beliefs of an audience in some predetermined way."[153] But this is a Herculean act because of its ambiguity which involves the ability to refute an opposing view in order to uphold your own view. However, Litfin encourages thus: "you will in some way identify the ideas you are discussing with the existing attitudes, beliefs, and values of your audience. What you want to refute will be related to the negative elements the audience belief system, while the ideas you want to advance will be related to the positive element of their belief system."[154] Apostle Paul adopted this precaution as recorded by the scripture in the Acts of Apostles (ch.17), in his speech delivered to the Athenians at Areopagus, but he failed later at his conclusion because he openly disagreed with what the general public – the Stoics and Epicureans philosophers of Athens and the foreigners held as a positive element of their belief system.

This road of persuasion which is sometimes argumentative in nature does not involve the ability to win an opponent or audience in a "shouting mania" rather it is the ability to convince an opponent through our behavior or attitude to things and through the rational line of thought. The most important thing in every argument is the ability to "win it" "and not the ability to lay down that point which you think that is convincing, without knowing you never lift a pin in moving the people along your line of thought". Hence Zimbardo remarks, "Persuasion is human communication designed by one source to influence other people by modifying their attitudes, or one or more of the components that make up an attitude."[155]

An effective persuasion is achieved as composite parts that make up a whole. Rhetoric as a major means of persuasion is of ancient origin, traced to the Greeks and Egyptians. The Greeks see it as an *organum* (tool) of democracy. The common citizens, who are not in power, often resort to rhetoric as a means to influence others by the power of argument instead of ranks and achievements. Aristotle presented three effective methods of persuasion (ethos, logos and pathos) but he ran short of few components that will aid persuasion to match the signs of all times.

Persuasion took a new shape in modern times when psychologists went into a serious research and study of the impact of persuasion. But before then, Hitler in his bid to melt out his wrath on the Jews was the first to develop a systematic way of persuasion in the modern time. This Nazi dictator established a ministry of propaganda whose function was to produce materials that would modify the attitudes of enemy forces against resistance and turn the German people against the Jews. This was the first wide-scale use of film as a tool of persuasion: powerful images and symbols were used to evoke strong emotions such as fear, disgust, and resignation.[156]

Fig. 11. 1 – *This poster is part of Hitler's propaganda campaign film the Germans used against the Jews. It reads, "Who buys from the Jews is a traitor".*

There are four major means of persuasion, which ranges from: ethos, pathos, evidence, and logos.

ETHOS

This is a careful blending of the speaker's character and a good accommodation of the audience by the speaker. The English equivalent of the Greek word Ethos is "character" – it is the way a speaker appears within a speech. Once the audience observes that the speaker has no good character, and that the speech is without any human feeling, they are bound to get uncomfortable with the speeches and therefore find it difficult to be convinced by the speaker. "A given communication is more effective if it appears to come from a highly credible source compared with one of lower credibility."[157] Cicero states, "…I also think his character sound – so much glory to the whole community do I see an outstanding orator who is also a man of worth."[158] That is why an orator is not just a talkative who talks without common sense; rather he is one who talks with full consciousness of the implication of whatever he is saying as he always keeps focused towards his goal.

The greatest mistake people make in oratory is the useless assumption or hasty conclusion that the audience already knows their character and therefore, finds no need of trying to prove to the audience their worth's again. Aristotle hence reassures that, "persuasion is achieved by the speaker's personal character when the speech is so spoken as to make us think credible. We believed good men more fully and more readily than others."[159]

Here is part of an inaugural address presented by John Kennedy on his day of swearing in as the president of the United State of America on the *20 January, 1961*. The concluding part of this speech is an embodiment of ethical proofs:

1. In your hands, my fellow citizens, more than mine, will rest the final success or failure of our course. Since this country was founded, each generation of Americans has been summoned to give testimony to its national loyalty. The graves of young Americans who answered the call to service surround the globe.

2. Now the trumpet summons us again – not as a call to bear arms, though arms we need – not as a call to battle, though embattled we are – but a call to bear the burden of a long twilight struggle, year in and year out, "rejoicing, patient in tribulation" – a struggle against the common enemies of man: tyranny, poverty, disease and war itself.

3. Can we forge against these enemies a grand and global alliance, North and South, East and West, that can assure a more fruitful life for all mankind? Will you join in the historic effort?

4. In the long history of the world, only a few generations have been granted the role of defending freedom in its hour of maximum danger. I do not shrink from this responsibility – I welcome it. I do not believe that any of us would exchange place with any other people other generation. The energy, the faith, the devotion which we bring to this endeavour will light our country and all who serve it – and the glow from that fire can truly light the world.

5.   And so, my fellow Americans: Ask not what your country can do for you – ask what you can do for your country.

6.   My fellow citizens of the world: Ask not what American will do for you, but what together we can do for the freedom of man.

7.   Finally, whether you are citizens of America or citizens of the world, ask of us here the same high standards of strength and sacrifice which we ask of you. With a good conscience our only sure reward, with history the final judge of our deeds, let us go forth to the land we love, asking his blessing and his help, but knowing that here on earth God's work must truly be our own.[160]

President John Kennedy in this address carefully blended and exposed the different facts and facets of his character. He also painted his character to the extent that it glows to the attraction of all who come across this address.

Paragraph 1, is a careful picture of Kennedy's love for his country (patriotism) and his modesty, while paragraph 2 is a sure sign of his life full of empathy. In paragraph 3, he radiates in sympathy – that is his concern for others. While in paragraph 4, a courageous and dedicated man (which are good qualities of a good leader), are shown. Paragraph 7, represents the climax of the address where he flashes his moral standard and his great religiosity. A speech organized in this nature can pull and move people to action (persuade) regardless of the formal or the real life of the speaker.

PATHOS
Emotion is an English equivalent of pathos. In modern scientific usage, the term emotion has multi-dimensional references that include: verbally expressible; subjective experiences; concomitant internal physiologic changes; and observable motor behavior (e.g. facial expression, gesture, posture). These fundamental aspects are richly documented

in human oral, written and artistic traditions.[161] Thus, Aristotle defined emotions as all those feelings that so change men as to affect their judgments, and that are also attended by pain or pleasure.[162] However, Adolf Hitler an oratory giant maintained a similar view when he said that: Only a storm of hot passion can turn the destinies of people.[163] Moreover, emotion suppresses reason in order to take precedence over every actions of man.

VARIOUS TYPES OF EMOTION

Anger:
Anger is a spontaneous emotion that arises in an individual, usually accompanied with pain, sorrow, anxiety and can even lead to dread.

A man gets angry depending on his disposition, he can be angry when he thinks that he is neglected, wronged, mocked, marginalized or disappointed, when faced with failure, and so on. Thus, each man is predisposed, by the emotion now controlling him, to his own particular anger.

An orator therefore having been at home with various things that can arouse the emotion of anger in people will have to speak so as to bring his audience into the right frame of mind that will dispose them to respond to such emotion. More so, he should also be able to make the audience cheerful at will, when anger is no more necessary.

Fear:
Fear is a painful or disturbing feeling due to mental picture of danger or of a strange thing yet to come, already at hand, or the remembrance of past evil.

"Fear is caused by whatever we feel has great power of destroying us, or of harming us in ways that tend to cause us great pain."[164] Fear starts in the mind and later reflects in actions. It is usually aroused when one sits back to reflect on past experiences, or when one begins to construct a strange picture that can initiate it. It arises "from either the perils of individuals or those shared by all: that of private origin goes deeper but universal fear also is to be trace to a similar source."[165]

Thus, people fear when they do hear of war or any form of terrorism. They fear death or anything that might lead to it. They fear lack of freedom. They fear people who are superior to them or who have the capability to harm them. In this age of anxiousness, people even fear to be in quiet places, fear about nemesis, or past evil.

On the part of the orator, with the requisite knowledge about fear, that can necessitate that, "it is advisable that the audience should be frightened, the orator must make them feel that they really are in danger of something, pointing out that it has happened to others who were stronger than they are, and is still happening and will continue to happen, at the hands of unexpected people in an expected form and at an unexpected time."[166]

Shame:
This is feeling of disturbance, when one thinks of certain things that might have happened, or are happening or yet to happen while considering the disgraceful consequences involved.

Sometime people feel ashamed of bad things that happen to people with whom they are associated. They fear to be disgraced, discredited, distrusted, and dishonored by people who admire them, those whom they admire, those from whom they seek admiration, those who compete with them, those whose opinion they respect and those who are related to them in one way or another.

People do as much as they can to avoid shame in this life. Aristotle once recounts the story of a poet, Antiphon, who was to be cudgeled to death by order of Dionysus. When he saw those who were to perish with him covering their faces as they went through the gates, he asked them thus, "why do you cover your faces? Is it lest some of these spectators should see you tomorrow?"

Given this, the orator should know when and how to stir the emotion of shame, especially among boastful audience. However, much care should be taken with this emotion, lest you might get disappointed with revolts from the audience.

Pity/Compassion:
This is sad and sympathetic feeling caused by the sight of suffering or trouble by others who do not deserve it, or when it seems to us that such emotions will come to us sooner or later.

Such painful and destructive evils that elicit compassion include: death in its various forms, bodily injuries, afflictions, old age, diseases, and lack of food. The problems due to chance are: friendlessness (it is a pitiful thing to be torn away from friends and companions) deformity, weakness, mutilation, evil coming from a source from which good ought to have come; and the frequent repetition of such misfortunes."[167] We also feel much pity when we find ourselves helpless in the face of a preceding evil happening or yet to happen to others.

Having known the nature of pity and its gravity, orators who excel most in stirring pity are those who heighten the effect of their words with suitable gestures, tones, dressing, etc. They make the world seem like crumbling through their words just to get the right emotion they desire to achieve.

Envy or Jealousy:
Envy or jealousy is the painful feeling at the sight of good fortunes of others. Thus Cicero has it that "men's private gains breed jealousy, while their zeal for others' service is applauded ... the emotion of jealousy is by far the fiercest of all and needs as much energy for its repression as for its stimulation."[168]

The competitive spirit is the arch conceiver of envy because people often do not envy those they have nothing to compete with. People normally envy their equals and, those who once were beneath them. Generally everybody aims at what is good or best, and majority pursue good things at all costs.
That is why ambitious men, wealthy men, small-minded men, are too jealous of the wiser, wealthier prosperous or great men because each man will always want to be the best. Thus, Cicero opined in consonance with this idea that, if these advantages (wealth, wisdom, prosperity and other goodies) are to be made full for jealousy, it should before all be pointed out that they were not the fruit of merit; next that they even came by vice and wrongdoing. Finally, that man's desires, though creditable and impressive enough are still exceeded by his arrogance and disdain.[169]

Love:
This is the emotion that goes with a very strong affection for others or for self in extreme cases. Friends can be in love with one another. People get in love with people they don't know before or even discussed with before. People can love

others because of the way they talk, dress, walk, sing, look, behave, eat or even for no reason at all.

An orator should strive to win the love of his audience in other to buy their will. To win the audience' love, act in the way that will make them look upon you as one upholding their interests and holding-out of a hope of advantage to come in more effective way than the recital of past benefit. You must struggle to reveal the presence, (in the cause you are upholding) of some merit or usefulness, and to make it plain that the man for whom you are to win his love, in no respect was consulted of his own interests and did nothing at all from any personal motive.[170]

THE EMOTIONAL STATE OF THE SPEAKER

It is most difficult to discover an object which causes an emotion when it is itself static. A good speaker should be sentimental, flexible and able to mimic in order to get his desired ends.

If you want your audience to cry, begin to cry, change your eye color and pretend to be drying your tears; if you want them to laugh, start laughing; if it is smile, start smiling; if you want them to clap, stir them to do so. If you want them to sing your praise act as a brave man, if you want them to be angry or to be sympathetic change your facial appearance by frowning it and you have the whole work done. "For it is impossible for the listener to feel indignation, hatred or ill-will, to be terrified of anything or reduced to tears of compassion, unless all those emotions which the advocate would inspire in the arbitrator are visibly stamped or rather branded on the advocate himself."[171]

Furthermore, Cicero adds, "I give you my word that I never tried by means of a speech, to arouse either indignation or compassion, either ill-will or hatred, in the minds of a tribunal, without being really stirred myself, as I worked upon their minds by the very feeling to which I was seeking to prompt them. For it is not easy to succeed in making an arbitrator angry with the right party, unless he first sees you on fire with hatred yourself; nor will making him hate the right party, unless you have shown him the tokens of your own grief by word, sentiment, tone of voice, look and by loud lamentation. For just as to be capable of generating flame without the application of a spark, so also there is no mind so ready to absorb an orator's influence, as to be inflammable when the assailing speaker is not himself aglow with passion."[172] It is only an orator who had certified himself as armed with all emotional and mental weapons who can dare his audience emotionally, lest his speech gets boring and his audience also gets weary of listening. Thus, these emotions can all be learned by every orator who is dedicated do so.

EVIDENCE:
Evidence is the presence of an undisputable reality. It is that which shines out to show the presence of something. By evidence we mean those known facts that guide us to other facts. It is simply whatever supports the truth claim. For any statement to be factual, there must be some evidence associated with it. This is because the one who claims to have the fact might be influenced by some conditions which make those facts questionable. Evidence is a tangible backup to a stated fact. Thus, there is little or no fact without verification and verification serves as evidence to facts. Hence William James, in his essay "Pragmatism" opined: Truth lives for the most part on a credit system. Our thoughts and beliefs 'pass," so long as nothing challenges them, just as banknotes pass so

long as nobody refuses them. But this all points to direct face-to-face verification somewhere, without which the fabric of truth collapses like a financial system with no cash basis whatever. You accept my verification of one thing, I yours. We trade on each other's truth. But beliefs verified concretely by *somebody* are the posts of the whole superstructure.[173]

Since evidence has so many roles to play in the part of giving us the truthfulness and factuality of anything, then it forms a good tool for persuasion. It helps an orator to speak with sureness, demonstrability, certitude, certainty, clarity, accuracy, exactitude, precision, sharpness, and distinctness. These evidences are what feed a reasonable ear and also attract the attention and reasoning of man.

Remember that your argument will require the careful use of evidence. It will succeed if you can use illustration and analysis to demonstrate the reasonableness of your claims. Do not choose a subject for a persuasive speech/essay that will require you to depend only on emotional appeal. There must be factual evidence which you already know or discovered through research. There are many types of evidence as discussed below:

VERIFIABLE EVIDENCE:
Speakers should be mindful not to convince their audience with weak and unverifiable statements which often make them kidding speakers. They should make sure their arguments are stuffed with evidence; facts, experimental results, figures, authoritative backups. Let what we present as facts remain those things that can be validated, corroborated, or verified. A person can hardly claim to have a fact without the second witness who is the verifier. So, the speaker should talk within the content of facts so that the audience's verification will enhance the acceptability of his speech.

Orators are advised to think before speaking in order to be able to harness their points in such a way that their facts could be verified by any reasonable mind around. Truth is one of those verifiable facts worth relying on and one should try as much as possible to get the unadulterated truth from the right source, namely from proven authorities in specific fields.

AUTHORITATIVE EVIDENCE:

Speakers should make sure that they are effectively garnishing every part of their speech with clear evidence. This clear evidence can only be achieved by a second observer or by referring to authorities who might be upholding such views too. An authority is one who is specially knowledgeable in a particular field – He is a master. A professor of a University is in the right place to set up a proposition about a particular course of study. But in this particular situation, *we are not talking about people who are jacks of all trade and masters of none.* We are rather talking about people who are expert in their areas of specialization.

QUALITIES OF AUTHORITATIVE OPINION

Mental Fitness:
Before a person can be an authority, he must be psychologically or mentally fit so that he can produce a qualitative knowledge.

Unprejudiced:
Some authorities find it difficult to say certain truths, because it might be to their own detriment. They therefore say certain things that might actually be false. Thus, an authority should be unprejudiced.

Must Have Evidence:
The authority should be the one who talks out of personal experience or other concrete evidence. Once an authority discusses matters without evidence, there is the possibility of being wrong.

Up-to-date Knowledge:
Any authority who doesn't know the recent development in his field is invariably not a competent authority.

Restricted Field of Specialty:
When an authority moves into a matter that does not pertain to his field, he is invariably not an authority in that field and therefore may be proved wrong.

Sincerity:
When an authority is not saying the truth, even if the matter is in relation to his field, he ceases to be a reliable authority.

LOGOS:
This involves being able to talk reasonably by use of well refined logic. From the Greek word "logos" we get the English "Logic", which refers to; appeals to reason, common sense, general knowledge, and scientific research. Though traditionally, logic is philosophically based yet we use it in our day to day life in our conversations, planning, decisions and many other facets of our life. Logic therefore is a very important tool for oratory, and to understand this well, let us explore of reasoning patterns in logic.

INDUCTIVE REASONING
This is a method of reasoning from a part to a whole, from particulars to generals, or from the individual to the universal. It can also be defined as a logical process in which connection is made between particulars or facts in order to

come to a generalization about them. It starts from known to unknown. It concerns test for strength and weakness, and as much may be evaluated as strong or weak according to the degree of likelihood or probability which premises confer upon conclusion.

Factors that can make Inductive Arguments strong:[174]

Appeal to authority: Example:
X is a reliable authority on Y
X seriously supports Y
Therefore, Y.

Appeal to Analogy: Example:
B behaves like C in certain conditions
B has property A
So, C has property A also.

Appeal to Enumeration: Example:
Drogba is the best African Footballer in the years 1999, 2003 and 2007.
So Drogba will be the best African Footballer in the year 2011.
Or The Nigerian Population is 20,000 in 1990, 70,000 in 1995, 190,000 in 2007. So it will be 220,000 in 2010.

Furthermore, every inductive argument is characterized by an inductive leap, namely, the little jump to generalization once few facts are gathered. This leap is determined by the nature of the subject and how many facts at hand. In an inductive argument like:

A short Lady was hostile to me in 1997.
A four-foot man was hostile thrice with my friend.
A short man was hostile to me again yesterday.

You can observe then from this example that since the argumentator above here have gathered few facts about short people, he is move to leap into generalization that; short people are hostile, without further inquiries. The ability to make good connections and to gather facts makes a good argument.

DEDUCTIVE REASONING

This is method of reasoning from general to particular and is the most common form of reasoning in argument. It is a logical process in which you make connections between a generalization (major premise), a fact (minor premise), and a conclusion. The deductive argument involves the claim that its premises provide conclusive grounds. It is impossible for its conclusion to be false while its premises are true.

Possible Features of a Valid Deductive Argument:
- Deductive argument can be possibly valid when all of its premises and conclusion are in fact true.
- A valid argument can also have false premises and a true conclusion.
- It is also possible to have a valid argument with false premises and a false conclusion.

Possible Features of Invalid Deductive Arguments:
- It is possible to have an invalid argument with true premises and a true conclusion.
- It is possible to have an invalid argument with at least one false premise and a false conclusion.
- It is also possible to have an invalid argument with true premises and a false conclusion.

Deductive Reasoning is most often expressed in the enthymeme. Enthymeme is a syllogism which is usually cast in a more conversational form and in which is missing either the major or the minor premise most of the time, an enthymeme is identifiable by words such as because, since, for, therefore, so thus, and hence, which signal either the conclusion or the support for an argument.

AVOIDANCE OF FALLACIES IN REASONING

Ordinarily, there can only be one truth and no other. Truth has no adulteration. It is the correspondence of thought to reality. The law of contradiction states that something cannot be and be at the same time. Any statement in logic which is not true is a fallacy.

Fallacy as a word is used in several distinct senses. It is sometimes used to indicate any mistake idea or false belief. For the logicians, the term 'fallacy", is used for arguments which may be psychologically persuasive, although incorrect. Fallacy is an error in reasoning. They are usually caused by human errors like: deceiving oneself, oversimplification, hasty conclusion, irrelevancies, dishonesty and being too emotional. The ability of one to avoid fallacies in argument increases the power to persuade and save one from the disgrace of being pinned down by an opponent in a law court or debate. There are many types of fallacy. Here are some of the major fallacies:

Argumentum Ad Baculum (Appeal to Force)

Argument Ad Hominem (Arguments Directed to the Man)

Argument Ad Hominem (Abusive)

The Art of Oratory

Argument Ad Hominem (Circumstantial)

Argument Ad Misericodiam (Appeal to Pity)

Argument Ad Populum (Appeal to popular sentiment)

Argument Ad Verecundiam (Appeal to Authority)

Argument Ad Ignoratiam (Appeal to Ignoraance)

Ignorantio Elenchi (Irrelevant Conclusion)

Appeal to Tradition:

Argument *Ad Dictum simpliciter* (Hasty Generalization/Converse Accident)

Petition Principii (Begging the Question)

The Non-Causa Pro Causa (No cause for cause)

Black-or-white Fallacy (Fallacy of false Alternatives)

Straw Man Fallacy

Slippery Slope Fallacy

Complex Question

Rhetorical Question

Ignoring the Question

Stereotyping

False Analogy

Genetic Fallacy

Guilt by Association

Division

Poisoning the Well

Red Herring

Special Pleading (double standard)

Fallacy of Equivocation

Fallacy of Accent

Non Sequitor

In summary, the persuader is a lamp bearer in the dark, he leads the audience to the direction he wishes, and therefore, every persuasion must have a concrete objective and should be able to proffer solutions. When your job as a persuader has been done, it will cast a spell on your audience, which will make it difficult for them not to follow your line of thought. Hence, audiences are usually vulnerable at the hands of good persuaders.

The Art of Oratory

Justin C. Nzekwe

CHAPTER TWELVE

HOW TO USE A MICROPHONE

The advent of microphone in 1970 by Dr. Lee DeForest in conjunction with the amplifiers, speakers, and other accessories was like a relief to olden speakers who out of lack of such an aid to amplify their voices when delivering speeches shout to the peak of their voices so as to be heard.

Microphone is now almost ubiquitous as it can be found in the studios, churches, auditorium, telephone and other mini or micro-computers, etc. It is an instrument that receives sound and is capable of transmitting, amplifying and magnifying the sound that comes across it. Even though the microphone does all these functions, yet it cannot be a substitute for good vocal expression. It is like a computer that operates with the principle of 'garbage in, garbage out'. Microphone gives you back or gives to your audience through its speakers whatever you have given to it; if you talk louder, it will sound louder, if you talk mildly, it will sound mildly. The whole emotions of a speaker are also represented by the microphone as it receives them verbally.

TYPES OF MICROPHONE
There are three major types of microphone. Though they do the same work of transmitting sounds but their uses and importance vary depending on the occasions at hand. The major types of microphone may include:

The Lavaliere microphone
The hand held microphone
The stationary microphone

THE LAVALIERE MICROPHONE

This is the type of microphone that can allow a speaker to freely move or walk around with both hands free to perform gestures.

The Lavalieres are usually clipped to the speaker's clothing – either on the lapel or tie. Therefore the dressing of the speaker matters a lot for the lavaliere user. He can either wear a suit, tie, jacket or any blouse that opens in the front as long as the lavaliere can be fastened firmly on it.

Usually, lavalieres are either wired or wireless. The handling of the wireless needs more precaution. The wireless lavaliere has a holder for batteries or a transmitter pack which can be clipped at the back side of clothing; either on the belt or waistband, or placed in a pocket to enable the transmitter receive signals without any interference.

The month piece of a lavaliere also be attached in such a way that it be safe from all external interferences, like; being interfered by the cloth weaving or similar obstructions. It should be placed in such a way that it does not make contact with the buttons, jewelries, and even the strands of hair as the sound from these can be amplified and transmitted. This, of course, may cause huge distraction to the audience.

HAND HELD MICROPHONE

This is a type of microphone that can permit the speaker to walk about while holding it in one hand. It gives the speaker the grace of using one hand of gestures. It also gives the speaker the total control over his volume depending on the distance from the mouth.

When the speaker draws the mic very close to the mouth, a different sound is produced. As much as the distance is increased or reduced, the volume varies.

The hand held mic can either be wireless or wired. When it is wireless, it permits the free movement of the speaker but not outside the wave length of the mic. Once the speaker moves outside the mic's wavelength, the signal drops and the microphone will be unable to pick up any sound.

In the case of a wired hand held microphone, the speaker can move a little further but is cautioned never to trip off the connection by moving further than the wire or cord could permit.

THE STATIONARY MICROPHONE

This is the type of microphone that is usually attached to the lectern or to the props. It helps the speaker to use both hands for gestures and also gives a total control of the sound and volume to a speaker.

The speaker can control the volume either by drawing closer to the mic or by allowing a reasonable distance.

The speaker is also permitted to use any kind of gesture he wishes with both hands without any hindrance from the mic.

HOW TO POSITION A MICROPHONE

Every microphone has what is known as a "pick up range". This is the area or range where the mic can receive a sound signal. Some microphones have a particular range within which the mic can focus to receive a sound (called "directional" range). Other mics require no particular range to focus for them to receive sound, (and is known as "omnidirectional").

DISTANCE

The clearness and distinctness of sound from a mic is achieved depending on the distance of the mic from the source of sound. The subject sound and not the ambient noise is what matters in the use of a microphone, hence the necessity of proper placement.

Fig. 12. 1: Example of a directional mic where the pickup pattern is said to be "cardioid".

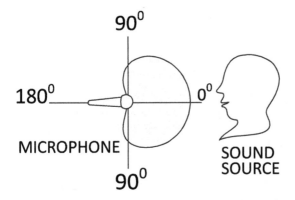

The diagram illustrates how this particular mic can receive sound- the range at which a sound can flow into it. Any sound that is not within this range is automatically lost or distorted.

When you are using a hand held or stationary mic, make sure that the sound that emanates from your mouth is perpendicular to your lips, face and teeth. Hence, you need to orient your face so that your voice is directed to the pick-up range of the mic.

Most lavaliere mics work best when placed eight to 10 inches below the chin ideally, in the centre. In the situation where you are using a slide, attach the mic in the direction of the slide, since you'll be focusing at the slides from time to time as you speak.

Remember that if you place the lavaliere mic too low, it will not pick every sound you give out. And also, when you place it too high, it will create an active and passive spots when you move your head during speech. So try to know the length of your active spots for proper placement and use.

PHASE PROBLEM:
In a situation where there is more than one mic and more than one sound, there is usually the possibility of the sound waves interfering with each other. The problem is a result of the same sound source, picked up from different mics placed at slightly different distances.

Phase problem can be avoided by your ability to raise your voice loud so as to stand out over the other sound/noises, compared to the other sounds in the mic's vicinity or range. For instance in live singing performance, with floor monitors on stage, you must be very close to the mic to ensure that your voice is louder than the sound coming from the monitor. Another example is in an interview situation in which two people each has a hand-held mic; when one person talks they are picked up by both mics and the resulting interference creates a phasing effect. The speaker is expected to reduce the voice and speak directly to his hand-held mic.

PROXIMITY EFFECT
The proximity effect is all down to the laws of physics, and may be a benefit or a problem depending on how it is handled. Speakers and singers use proximity effect to vary or alter the tone of their voices when they speak or sing. This depends on the distance on the distance of the mouth from the mic at any circumstance. The proximity effect can also serve as an equalizer because when the speaker draws very close to the mic, he produces a bassy sound

The pop shield in between the speaker and mic and the reasonable distance maintained by the speaker makes it difficult for the sound to be affected by a proximity effect unless in a recording musical instrument where it is deliberately allowed.

GUIDELINES FOR CHOOSING A MICROPHONE[175]
There are many guidelines that can help one avoid the mistake of making a wrong choice of a microphone. Each studio, hall auditorium, church or other related places should have a microphone most suitable for it. Christopher Rath Stated three major guidelines for a better choice of microphone:

- ✓ By the right mic for your voice. Go to the musical equipment store and try a selection of vocal mics. Select the one most suited to your voice. When trying each mic, make sure the amplifier you are singing or speaking through has its EQ set flat (i.e, no extra treble, bass, reverb, etc.) so that you can be sure you are hearing the real differences between each mic.

✓ Buy the mic most suited to the physical situation where you will be using the mic. For example, if you will be using the mic in live setting, don't purchase a mic intended for use in a recording studio.

✓ Learn to use the mic properly. A high quality, properly chosen device will only produce a desirable result if it is properly used. The manufacture's data sheet for the mic is generally the best starting point in determining how to use a specific mic.

It is also good to take cognizance of the fact that good microphone cannot speak or sing for you. It will only produce what you have given to it just as it received it from you.

MOUNTING A MICROPHONE

Among the mistakes people make is the *a priori* assumption of how to use microphone or how to set or mount it. The poor mounting of microphone creates unpredictable or uncountable problems while a well mounted one makes for a quality presentation by whoever uses it.

There are some pertinent precautions for mounting a mic. Those precautions include:

Safety: Keep your mic in a cold place, safe from wet, falls and knocks.

Security: Make sure the cable of the mic is secured to avoid being tripped off during any presentation.

Shield: Try to shield the mic from unwanted noise either from careless handling, vibrations, wind and other related factors.

Positioning: The mic should be positioned correctly to the right direction at any given time.

SOME METHODS OF MOUNTING A MICROPHONE

There are many modern ways of mounting a mic. This work will consider the two popular ways: The boom stand and the table-top stand.

THE BOOM STAND

The boom stand is a popular type of microphone stand usually with three legs and many other features that aid in adjusting and readjusting it. It stands vertically with a horizontal crossing at the top which serves as the clamp. It is an all-purpose stand and probably the most suitable for different occasions.

For an effective service by the boom stand, there are some necessary precautions:

- To prevent the stand from falling, always position the horizontal part to extend directly above one of the stand's legs.

- Do not over tighten the clamps so as to make it easier to adjust or re-adjust when it is inevitable.

- Do not stand on the legs lest you fall or spoil the stand.

- Apply your common sense in the use of such sensitive instrument.

TABLE TOP STAND

This is shorter form of a boom stand. The table stand needs the support of the table to raise the height of the stand. It usually doesn't have legs, but rather a base to enable it stand firm. They are mostly used in the case where the speaker uses a table or where the speaker needs to sit and talk. The use of common sense will bring out the best in the service of the stand.

SHOCK ABSORPTION
In the use of a microphone, any sound that is not from the speaker is unwanted and therefore should be avoided. This is because such noise brings distractions and distortion of any message communicated through the mic.

These noises are usually as a result of vibrations of the stand or the inability of the stand to grip the mic firmly. Some of these noises can rightly be avoided by firm tightening of the clamp and also by a good isolation of the mic from the vibration, by padding the mic with foam or an elastic suspension.

KNOWING HOW TO TURN THE MICROPHONE ON AND OFF
One of the first things a speaker learns in the use of a mic is how to turn the microphone on or off at the right time can make a mess of even a good presentation. Here are some right times to off a mic.

> ➤ When the speaker is about to cough or sneeze.

- ➢ If the sound system starts acting up by distorting, squealing, producing a lot of static, howling, clicking, cutting-in-and-out, going from loud to soft sounds.

- ➢ During a break many users of a lavaliere mic have found their confidential discussions being heard by the audience or the unwanted sounds of lavatories being communicated to the audience. This is usually as a result of leaving the mic on during a break.

THE NEED FOR A SOUND CHECK

If you are to use a microphone for any live performance, always try to make a sound check to avoid being embarrassed by the microphones. Many technicians can be trusted in the matters of setting the mic while many are not to be trusted.

Come earlier than your audience and get a person to move to the hall or any other place you are going to deliver your speech and hear you speak in order to assess the sound quality of the mic.

It is good to understand that it is the neophytes that test the mic by blowing air or tapping the mic. Better say, 'hello', good day' or any other thing relevant without distracting while testing a mic.

THE GENERAL RULES OF MICROPHONE TECHNIQUE

- Know the directional characteristics of the mic you use.

- Don't cover the mic with your hand lest it causes unwanted feedbacks.

- Make sure you sound check the mic prior to any deliver.

- Orient the mic so that your voice travels directly into the pickup pattern to the mic.
- Learn to turn the mic off or on at the right time, to save current, and effective discharge of duty.

- When the mic is used by more than one person, the whole voices should contribute an equal share of sound within the pick-up range.

- Hold the mic firmly to avoid vibrations and the picking up of unwanted noise.

- Protect the mic from the direction of the wind to avoid noise and the mic developing problems.

- The mic should not face a monitor or a loud speaker to avoid sound reversal and an extreme introduction of unwanted sound.

- Don't draw the mic so close to the mouth to avoid a popping sound effect of too far to avoid producing a weak and faint sound.

- Do not bang or drop a mic carelessly because mics use fragile mechanism to transform the sound to electrical signal translation process, and its mechanism may be damaged by physical shock.

The Art of Oratory

It is good to notice that the microphone is a fragile and sensitive instrument and so, a great deal of care should be taken in handling it. Also there is a great need of one using a microphone to make use of his or her good common sense in the use of a microphone.

MAINTAINANCE OF MICROPHONE

Every microphone has a maintenance kit attached to it or maintenance instruction if it is brought new from the dealers. Here are some of the general maintenance principles that might interest you if you wish to extend the life of your mic set.

- Do not expose the mic to a very high temperature, humidity, dust, physical shocks etc.

- Do not handle the mic at the cable as it might develop the problem of partial contact in the mic.

- Do not blow air into the mic because the diaphragm is only designed to respond to sound waves and not air.

- Always replace dead batteries to avoid destroying the battery contacts.

- Turn of the mic when not in use to save power.

- Make good use of the phantom power.

- When you notice weakness in the functioning of the mic, the first step is to clean the diaphragm. If it continues contact the manufacturers.

It is good to understand that these principles are created to prolong the life of your set and some of them serve as a first aid to the mic set. But in some situation beyond control, remember that electric devices are dangerous to those who can't manage them. Try to keep your supplier or manufacturer in contact at difficult or confusing moments.

The Art of Oratory

CHAPTER THIRTEEN

HOW TO CONCLUDE YOUR SPEECH

This is the time when the entire information you have communicated throughout the speech are knitted together to form a meaning which is whole and specific. According to Aristotle, a good conclusion "merely reminds us of what has been said already."[176]

At the conclusion of a speech is where the audiences are brought back to life. Some audience might be carried away by life's necessities, some might be distracted by one thing or another, some might dose off or might be mopping without listening. But at the approach of the conclusion, they once more pick up a fresh interest.

If you had made a wonderful presentation, the presentation can easily be marred by a bad conclusion. Also a good conclusion can rewrite the impression formally created by an amateur presenter. In conclusion lies the merit and demerit of any speech. Litfin argues that, "a strong conclusion can compensate for previous weaknesses in the speech. Perhaps your introduction was less interesting than it might have been; or perhaps your structure was cloudy, your transitions weak, or your supporting material too vague. But if your audience is still listening to you at the end of the speech, you can partially overcome these shortcomings with a strong conclusion."[177]

A lot of people who are emotional or with shorter memory go home with the last fun or quotation or mood of the speaker. It is the delicate time of the speech delivery. And it should command the highest percussion of the speeches. So therefore, "like a great fireworks show, you save your best for last. Yes, you begin with great attention – getting material, but the "big bang" is for the finish."[178] Archbishop Fulton recommends that "the conclusion of a talk must be strong, inspiring and elevating and I would spend almost as much time on it as on many points in the lectures…."[179]

It is good you dispose your audience towards the conclusion of your speech, but you should avoid as much as you can using words like "in conclusion", "Finally", or "conclusively". Good speakers create awareness of their conclusion by changing the tone of their voices, by giving a kind of summary to their speeches, by using some words which arouse the inquisitiveness of the audience the more or some other methodology. In other words, "there should always be a clear awareness that you have *finished;* you have come full circle; you have arrived where you set out to go. This is what the speech has been all about, and if it has not been entirely clear as of yet, it finally becomes clear here."[180]

Some inexperienced speakers have the wrong culture of disposing the audience for conclusion as many times as possible, this makes the audience get bored of their speeches. Other categories of inexperienced speakers are those who arrive at the end of a speech without people knowing it is time. This instigates a lot of questions in the audience and even makes them regret coming to listen to you or may make them go home confused.

Furthermore, speeches should end with a challenge. "Challenge' here means leading people to do the purpose of your speech, like Mark Anthony of Julius Caesar who wants his audience to discover the truth of what he is saying and to move for action. In essence, before Mark Anthony could finish the speech, people have captured his purpose from different perspectives that they don't need to listen more before they can act. Thus Sherman comments, "Unfortunately, 'asking for more' was really a euphemism for failing to convey a clear picture of what I wanted my listeners to do."[181]

Never forget that the complexity and simplicity of your conclusion depends on that of the body of the speech; never derail from the message of which the body of the speech has communicated. More so, try not to as assume the function of the chairman of the occasion or that of the Master of the Ceremony (M.C) by jumping into words of thanks and gratitude at the end of your speech, rather finish humbly and walk out gently to your seat and your speech will do the rest for you. Get the following useful encouragement:[182]

- ✓ Be sure your finale mirrors and relates to your original purpose. It lets the audience know you satisfied that objective.

- ✓ Have only one ending. I've heard speakers use two or three conclusions that left the audience confused.

- ✓ End confidently. Never say, "That's about it," "And one more thing," or "oh I forget to mention.

SUGGESTED PRECAUTIONS TO BE TAKEN IN CONCLUDING A SPEECH

There are some suggested ways that can lead to an effective conclusion and which we must bear in mind in every speech delivery.

Climbing up and down the slope:
It is good you master your voice so that at the conclusion, it is expected you change your tone to depict conclusion and not just talking with the same tone throughout the speech.

Be content With What You Have:
This is not time to develop a new idea, even if you want to express yourself in a new way, strive not to import a new idea inside your speech. Let the conclusion be a sign post pointing toward the body of the speech.

Attempt Summary:
It is possible to use fresh words to give a vivid expression of what your speech is all about. Give a systematic review of your speech. It can be direct through overt and straight forward speech or it can be indirect with quotation and story.

Unveiling Your Speech:
This is the time where clarity and conciseness reign most in the speech. If this action is not done, you might end up leaving your audience more confused than they were before listening to you.

Humor can be Instrumental:
It is good to tell an interesting story which contains a lot of message to communicate pertaining to your speech. At this point Tom Anton Comments, "If you leave them laughing and applauding … an extremely positive impression about

you will remain." But if your entire speech has included humor, Tom recommends that you finish seriously. He further said, "This contrast will create a great impact. It will convey the fact that you believe in a lightened approach to the subject, but the result are very serious to you."[183]

Roundabout a Circle:
Start from the introduction and touch every bit of the point that you have to strike in order to make it fresh in the memory of your audience while you leave them.

You Can Apply an Emotion:
Your application of emotion inspires the audience and moves them to action immediately. Thus Cicero contended that, "there is no mind so ready to absorb an orator's influence, as to the inflammable when the assailing speaker is not himself aglow with passion."[184] So therefore a heart-touching anecdote helps you bring out your points and make a firm demand from your audience.

Give them a challenge:
Conclusion is where you challenge your audience to action in order for them to meet the aim of your speech delivery. Every speech delivery has a purpose which must be met in every speech delivery.

Add Your Opinion:
You can chip in your own suggestions or your own view in the matter being discussed in order to make your speech more natural and down to earth.

Strike the Middle in Matters of Time:
Let your conclusion not be more than 15 percent of the entire time given to you for your speech and let it not be less than 5 percent of the time. Make your conclusion a bit longer in

order to achieve within the range. Hence, Cicero encourages that, "the opening of a speech is unhurried, and none the less its closing should also be lingered and long drawn out."[185]

Curtail Excess:
Avoid using words like: "in conclusion". It is also a wrong disposition for you to use words like "Thank you" without *raison d'être*. Let words and sentences you use be precise and direct to the point.

SOME EXAMPLES OF CONCLUDING SPEECHES
The purpose of adapting some speeches of old delivered by great orators here is to help prospective speakers have examples of how speeches should be concluded. Most of these speeches are not perfect but they are among the best so far in history. Here are the examples:

EXAMPLE ONE:
The famous 'I have a dream' speech delivered before the thousands assemble on the Lincoln Memorial, Washington, on 28 August, 1963 by Martin Luther King Jr. An American clergymen militant, non-violet civil rights leader, and Negro integrated leader. Here is the concluding part of the speech.

I say to you today, my friends, so even though we face the difficulties of today and tomorrow. I still have a dream. It is a dream deeply rooted in the American dream.

I have a dream that one day this nation will rise up and live out the true meaning of its creed: "we hold these truths to be self-evident that all men are created equal." I have a dream that one day on the red hills of Georgia, the sons of former slave and the sons of former slave owners will be able to sit down together at a table of brothering with the heat of injustice and operation, will be transformed into an oasis of freedom and justice. I have a dream that my four children will one day live in a nation where they will not be judged by the color of their skin but by the content of their character. I have a dream today.

I have a dream that one day the state of Alabama, whose governor's lips are recently dripping with the words of interposition and nullification, will be transformed into a situation where little black boys and black girls will be able to join hands with little white boys and white girls and walk together as sisters and brothers. I have a dream today. I have a dream that one day every valley shall be exalted, every hill and mountain shall be made low, the rough places will be made plain, and the crooked places will be made straight, and the glory of the Lord shall be revealed, and all flesh shall see it together. This is our hope. This is the faith with which I return to the South. With this faith we will be able to hew out of the mountain of despair a stone of hope. With this faith we will be able to transform the jangling discords of our nation into a beautiful symphony of brotherhood. With this faith we will be able to work together, to pray together, to struggle together, to go to jail together, to stand up for freedom together, knowing that we will be free one day.

This will be the day when all of God's children will be able to sing with a new meaning, "My country, 'tis of thee, sweet land of liberty, of thee I sing. Land where my fathers died, land of the pilgrim's pride, from every mountainside, let freedom ring." And if America is to be a great nation, this must become true. So let freedom ring from the prodigious hilltops of New Hampshire. Let freedom ring from the mighty mountains of New York. Let freedom ring from the heightening Alleghenies of Pennsylvania! Let freedom ring from the snowcapped Rockies of Calorado! Let freedom ring from the curvaceous peaks of California! But not only that; Let freedom ring from Stone Mountain of Georgia! from Lookout Mountain of Tennessee! Let freedom ring from every hill and every molehill of Mississippi. From every mountainside, let freedom ring.

When we let freedom ring, when we let it ring every village and every hamlet, from every state and every city, we will be able to speech up that day when all of God's children – black men and white men, Jews and Gentiles, Protestants and Catholics – will be able to join hands and sing in the words of the old Negro spiritual, "Free at last! Free at last! Thank God Almighty, we are free at last!"

EXAMPLE TWO

A speech delivered by Napoleon- I [Bonaparte] a French emperor and general whose brilliant victories over Austrians and Russians made him practically the master of Europe. He addressed this speech to his soldiers on 27 March 1796 when entering Italy. Here is the concluding part of the speech:

Yes, soldiers, you have done much. But remains there nothing more to do? Shall it be said of us that we have conquered, but not now to make use of victory? Shall posterity reproach us with having found Capua in Lombardy? But I see you already hasten to arms. An effeminate response is tedious to you; the days which are lost to glory are lost to your happiness. Well, then, let us set forth! We have still forced marches to make, enemies to subdue, laurels to gather, injuries to revenge. Let those who have sharpened the daggers of civil war in France, who have dared to murder our ministers and burn our ships at Toulon tremble!

The hour of vengeance has struck; but let the people of all countries be free from apprehension; we are the friends of the people everywhere, and of those great men whom we have taken for our models. To restore the capital, to replace the status of the heroes who rendered it illustrations, to rouse the Roman people, stupefied by several ages of slavery – such will be the fruit of our victories. They will form an era for posterity. You will have the immortal glory of changing the face of the finest part of Europe. The French people, free and respected by the whole, will give to Europe a glorious peace, which for the last six years they have been making. You will then return to your homes and your county. Men will say, as they point you out, "He belongs to the army of Italy."

EXAMPLE THREE:

A speech delivered by Unachukwu Nnamdi Cyril, CCE a seminarian, secretary and Editor of Potential Leader Forum (POLEF). *This is titled BEING WHAT YOU ARE. He addressed this speech to the* graduating philosopher of Seat of Wisdom Seminary, Nigeria, 2008/2009 academic and formation year on the occasion of their class sent-forth party on 25 June, 2009. *Here is the concluding part of the speech:*

Dear brothers, we love you all, we appreciate you all, we cherish you all, we care for you all and we pray for you all. We say and mean all these for you because of what you are. Being what you are, in this context, is a reminder and also a call. And because we have seen and have experienced what you are, we remind and call on you to remain and be what you are. At your places of long apostolic work, be what you are; for those who will come back immediately, be what you are as you come back; For those who may not like to continue in the seminary system, be what you are wherever you find yourself; and for all of us collectively, let us be what we are in all that we do. It is in being what we are that our existence is evidenced. We are authentic and mature when we remain in the realm of being what we are.

It is on this note that your immediate younger brothers say thank you; the executives of NAPS say thank you; the entire body of NAPS say thank you, and finally, the whole members of 'POLEF' say thank you. May the creator of the universe grant us the grace and the strength to be what we are to the greater glory of his name and for our own good; Thanks and God bless you all.

EXAMPLE FOUR:
The speech delivered by Senator Barrack Obama, the first African American president of America, elected in 2008. A renowned lawyer and an Orator. He delivered this speech at the Constitution Centre Philadelphia, Pennsylvania. The speech was titled "a More Perfect Union. "Here is the concluding part of the speech:

I would not be running for President if I didn't believe with all my heart that this is what the vast majority of Americans want for this country. This union may never be perfect, but generation after generation has shown that it can always be perfected. And today, whenever I find myself feeling doubtful or cynical about this possibility, what gives me the most hope is the next generation – the young people whose attitudes and beliefs and openness to change have already made history in this election.

There is one story in particularly that I'd like to leave you with today – a story I told when I had the great honor of speaking on Dr. King's birthday at his home church, Ebenezer Baptist, in Atlanta.

The Art of Oratory

There is a young, twenty-three year old white woman named Ashley Baia who organized for our campaign in Florence, South Carolina. She had been working to organize a mostly African-American community since the beginning of this campaign, and one day she was at a roundtable discussion where everyone went around telling their story and why they were there.

And Ashley said that when she was nine years old, her mother got cancer. And because she had to miss days of work, she was let go and lost her health care. They had to file for bankruptcy, and that's when Ashley decided that she had to do something to help her mom.

She knew that food was one of their most expensive costs, and so Ashley convinced her mother that what she really liked and really to eat more than anything else was mustard and relish sandwiches. Because that was the cheapest way to eat.

She did this for a year until her mom got better, and she told everyone at the roundtable that the reason she joined our campaign was so that she could help the millions of other children in the country who want and need to help their parents too.

Now Ashley might have made a different choice. Perhaps somebody told her along the way that the source of her mother's problem were blacks who were on welfare and too lazy to work, or Hispanics who were coming into the country illegally. But she didn't. She sought out allies in her fight against injustice.

Anyway, Ashley finishes her story and then goes around the room and asks everyone else why they're supporting the campaign. They all have different stories and reasons. Many bring up a specific issue. And finally they come to this elderly black man who's been sitting there quietly the entire time. And Ashley asks him why he's there. And he does not bring up a specific issue. He does not say health care or the economy. He does not say education or the war. He does not say that he was there because of Barack Obama. He simply says to everyone in the room, "I am here because of Ashley."

I'm here because of Ashley," By itself, that single moment of recognition between that young white girl and that old black man is not enough. It is not enough to give health care to the sick, or jobs to the jobless, or education to our children.

But it is where we start. It is where our union stronger. And as so many generations have come to realize over the course of the two-hundred and twenty one years since a band of patriots signed that document in Philadelphia, that is where the perfection begins.

The Art of Oratory

APPENDIX

Appendix One

The speech delivered by Prime Minister David Cameron, the Prime Minister of the United Kingdom. He delivered this speech on June 2016, outside Downing Street following Britain's vote to leave the European Union. He announced his resignation as the Prime Minister of the Great Britain in this speech. Here is the full speech:

"Good morning everyone, the country has just taken part in a giant democratic exercise, perhaps the biggest in our history.

Over 33 million people from England, Scotland, Wales, Northern Ireland and Gibraltar have all had their say.

We should be proud of the fact that in these islands we trust the people for these big decisions.

We not only have a parliamentary democracy, but on questions about the arrangements for how we've governed there are times when it is right to ask the people themselves and that is what we have done.

The British people have voted to leave the European Union and their will must be respected.

I want to thank everyone who took part in the campaign on my side of the argument, including all those who put aside party differences to speak in what they believe was the national interest and let me congratulate all those who took part in the Leave campaign for the spirited and passionate case that they made.

The will of the British people is an instruction that must be delivered.

It was not a decision that was taken lightly, not least because so many things were said by so many different organisations about the significance of this decision.

So there can be no doubt about the result.

Across the world people have been watching the choice that Britain has made.

I would reassure those markets and investors that Britain's economy is fundamentally strong and I would also reassure Britons living in European countries and European citizens living here there will be no immediate changes in your circumstances.

There will be no initial change in the way our people can travel, in the way our goods can move or the way our services can be sold.

We must now prepare for a negotiation with the European Union.

This will need to involve the full engagement of the Scottish, Welsh and Northern Ireland governments to ensure that the interests of all parts of our United Kingdom are protected and advanced.

But above all this will require strong, determined and committed leadership.

I'm very proud and very honoured to have been Prime Minister of this country for six years.

I believe we've made great steps, with more people in work than ever before in our history, with reforms to welfare and education, increasing people's life chances, building a bigger and stronger society, keeping our promises to the poorest people in the world and enabling those who love each other

to get married whatever their sexuality, but above all restoring Britain's economic strength.

And I'm grateful to everyone who's helped to make that happen.

I have also always believed that we have to confront big decisions, not duck them.

That is why we delivered the first coalition government in 70 years, to bring our economy back from the brink.

It's why we delivered a fair, legal and decisive referendum in Scotland.

And it's why I made the pledge to renegotiate Britain's position in the European Union and to hold the referendum on our membership and have carried those things out.

I fought this campaign in the only way I know how, which is to say directly and passionately what I think and feel - head, heart and soul.

I held nothing back, I was absolutely clear about my belief that Britain is stronger, safer and better off inside the European Union and I made clear the referendum was about this and this alone - not the future of any single politician including myself.

But the British people have made a very clear decision to take a different path and as such I think the country requires fresh leadership to take it in this direction.

I will do everything I can as Prime Minister to steady the ship over the coming weeks and months but I do not think it would be right for me to try to be the captain that steers our country to its next destination.

This is not a decision I've taken lightly but I do believe it's in the national interest to have a period of stability and then the new leadership required.

There is no need for a precise timetable today but in my view we should aim to have a new prime minister in place by the start of the Conservative Party conference in October.

Delivering stability will be important and I will continue in post as Prime Minister with my Cabinet for the next three months.

The Cabinet will meet on Monday, the Governor of the Bank of England is making a statement about the steps that the Bank and the Treasury are taking to reassure financial markets.

We will also continue taking forward the important legislation that we set before Parliament in the Queen's Speech.

And I have spoken to Her Majesty the Queen this morning to advise her of the steps that I am taking.

A negotiation with the European Union will need to begin under a new prime minister and I think it's right that this new prime minister takes the decision about when to trigger Article 50 and start the formal and legal process of leaving the EU.

I will attend the European Council next week to explain the decision the British people have taken and my own decision.

The British people have made a choice, that not only needs to be respected but those on the losing side of the argument - myself included - should help to make it work.

Britain is a special country - we have so many great advantages - a parliamentary democracy where we resolve great issues about our future through peaceful debate, a great trading nation with our science and arts, our engineering and our creativity, respected the world over.

And while we are not perfect I do believe we can be a model for the multi-racial, multi-faith democracy, that people can come and make a contribution and rise to the very highest that their talent allows.

Although leaving Europe was not the path I recommended, I am the first to praise our incredible strengths.

I said before that Britain can survive outside the European Union and indeed that we could find a way.

Now the decision has been made to leave, we need to find the best way and I will do everything I can to help.

The Art of Oratory

I love this country and I feel honoured to have served it and I will do everything I can in future to help this great country succeed. Thank you very much."

Appendix Two
The famous 'I have a dream' speech delivered before the thousands assembled on the Lincoln Memorial, Washington, on 28 August, 1963 by Martin Luther King, an American clergyman, militant, non-violent civil rights leader, and Negro integrated leader.

I am happy to join with you today in what will go down in history as the greatest demonstration for freedom in the history of our nation.

Five score years ago, a great American, in whose symbolic shadow we stand today, signed the Emancipation Proclamation. This momentous decree came as a great beacon light of hope to millions of Negro slaves who had been seared in the flames of withering injustice. It came as a joyous daybreak to end the long night of captivity.

But one hundred years later, the Negro still is not free. One hundred years later, the life of the Negro is still sadly crippled by the manacles of segregation and the chains of discrimination. One hundred years later, the Negro lives on a lonely island of poverty in the midst of a vast ocean of material prosperity. One hundred years later, the Negro is still languished in the corners of American society and finds himself in exile in his own land. So we have come here today to dramatize a shameful condition.

In a sense we've come to our nation's Capital to cash a check. When the architects of our republic wrote the magnificent words of the Constitution and the Declaration of Independence, they were signing a promissory note to which every American was to fall heir.

This note was a promise that all men, yes, black men as well as white men, would be guaranteed the unalienable rights of life, liberty, and the pursuit of happiness.

It is obvious today that America has defaulted on this promissory note insofar as her citizens of colour are concerned. Instead of honouring this sacred obligation, America has given the Negro people a bad check; a check which has come back marked "insufficient funds."

But we refuse to believe that the bank of justice is bankrupt. We refuse to believe that there are insufficient funds in the great vaults of opportunity of this nation. So we have come to cash this check- a check that will give us upon demand the riches of freedom and the security of justice.

We have also come to this hallowed spot to remind America of the fierce urgency of now. This is no time to engage in the luxury of cooling off or to take the tranquilizing drug of gradualism.

Now is the time to make real the promises of democracy. Now is the time to rise from the dark and desolate valley of segregation to the sunlit path of racial justice. Now is the time to lift our nation from the quicksand of racial injustice to the solid rock of brotherhood. Now is the time to make justice a reality for all of God's children.

The Art of Oratory

It would be fatal for the nation to overlook the urgency of the moment. This sweltering summer of the Negro's legitimate discontent will not pass until there is an invigorating autumn of freedom and equality. Nineteen sixty-three is not an end, but a beginning. Those who hope that the Negro needed to blow off steam and will now be content will have a rude awakening if the nation returns to business as usual. There

will be neither rest nor tranquillity in America until the Negro is granted his citizenship rights. The whirlwinds of revolt will continue to shake the foundations of our nation until the bright day of justice emerges.

But there is something that I must say to my people who stand on the warm threshold which leads into the palace of justice. In the process of gaining our rightful place we must not be guilty of wrongful deeds. Let us not seek to satisfy our thirst for freedom by drinking from the cup of bitterness and hatred. We must forever conduct our struggle on the high plane of dignity and discipline. We must not allow our creative protest to degenerate into physical violence. Again and again we must rise to the majestic heights of meeting physical force with soul force.

The marvellous new militancy which has engulfed the Negro community must not lead us to a distrust of all white people, for many of our white brothers, as evidenced by their presence here today, have come to realize that their destiny is tied up with our destiny. And they have come to realize that their freedom is inextricably bound to our freedom. We cannot walk alone.

And as we walk, we must make the pledge that we shall march ahead. We cannot turn back. There are those who are asking the devotees of civil rights, "When will you be satisfied?"

We can never be satisfied as long as the Negro is the victim of the unspeakable horrors of police brutality.

We can never be satisfied as long as our bodies, heavy with the fatigue of travel, cannot gain lodging in the motels of the highways and the hotels of the cities.

We cannot be satisfied as long as the Negro's basic mobility is from a smaller ghetto to a larger one.

We can never be satisfied as long as our children are stripped of their selfhood and robbed of their dignity by signs stating "for whites only."

We cannot be satisfied as long as a Negro in Mississippi cannot vote and a Negro in New York believes he has nothing for which to vote.

No, no, we are not satisfied, and we will not be satisfied until justice rolls down like waters and righteousness like a mighty stream.

I am not unmindful that some of you have come here out of great trials and tribulations. Some of you have come fresh from narrow jail cells. Some of you have come from areas where your quest for freedom left you battered by the storms of persecution and staggered by the winds of police brutality. You have been the veterans of creative suffering. Continue to work with the faith that unearned suffering is redemptive.

Go back to Mississippi, go back to Alabama, go back to South Carolina, go back to Georgia, go back to Louisiana, go back to the slums and ghettos of our northern cities, knowing that somehow this situation can and will be changed. Let us not wallow in the valley of despair.

The Art of Oratory

I say to you today, my friends, so even though we face the difficulties of today and tomorrow, I still have a dream. It is a dream deeply rooted in the American dream.

I have a dream that one day this nation will rise up and live out the true meaning of its creed: "We hold these truths to be self-evident; that all men are created equal."

I have a dream that one day on the red hills of Georgia the sons of former slaves and the sons of former slave owners will be able to sit down together at the table of brotherhood.

I have a dream that one day even the state of Mississippi, a state sweltering with the heat of injustice, sweltering with the heat of oppression, will be transformed into an oasis of freedom and justice.

I have a dream that my four little children will one day live in a nation where they will not be judged by the colour of their skin but by the content of their character.

I have a dream today.

I have a dream that one day down in Alabama, with its vicious racists, with its governor having his lips dripping with the words of interposition and nullification, that one day right down in Alabama little black boys and black girls will be able to join hands with little white boys and white girls as sisters and brothers.

I have a dream today.

I have a dream that one day every valley shall be exalted, every hill and mountain shall be made low, the rough places will be made plain, and the crooked places will be made straight, and the glory of the Lord shall be revealed, and all flesh shall see it together.

This is our hope. This is the faith that I will go back to the South with. With this faith we will be able to hew out of the mountain of despair a stone of hope. With this faith we will be able to transform the jangling discords of our nation into a beautiful symphony of brotherhood.

With this faith we will be able to work together, to pray together, to struggle together, to go to jail together, to stand up for freedom together, knowing that we will be free one day.

This will be the day when all of God's children will be able to sing with new meaning, "My country 'tis of thee, sweet land of liberty, of thee I sing. Land where my fathers died, land of the Pilgrims' pride, from every mountainside, let freedom ring."

And if America is to be a great nation, this must become true. So let freedom ring from the prodigious hilltops of New Hampshire. Let freedom ring from the mighty mountains of New York. Let freedom ring from the heightening Alleghenies of Pennsylvania.

Let freedom ring from the snow-capped Rockies of Colorado. Let freedom ring from the curvaceous slopes of California. But not only that; let freedom ring from the Stone Mountain of Georgia. Let freedom ring from Lookout Mountain of Tennessee.

Let freedom ring from every hill and molehill of Mississippi. From every mountainside, let freedom ring.

And when this happens, and when we allow freedom ring, when we let it ring from every village and every hamlet, from every state and every city, we will be able to speed up that day when all of God's children, black men and white men, Jews and gentiles, Protestants and Catholics, will be able to join hands and sing in the words of the old Negro spiritual, "Free at last! Free at last! Thank God Almighty, we are free at last!"

Appendix Three

A speech delivered by Unachukwu Nnamdi Cyril CCE, as a seminarian, secretary and editor of Potential Leaders Forum (POLEF). This is titled BEING WHAT YOU ARE. He addressed this speech to the graduating philosophers of Seat of Wisdom Seminary, Nigeria, 2008/2009 academic and formation year on the occasion of their class sent-forth party on 25th day of June, 2009.

Dear brother in Christ, it is a thing of joy to be in your midst this day. As we all know, we have gathered here this day to thank God for His kindness to us these four years and beyond in our seminary training. We have gathered here this day to say to ourselves lots of congratulatory messages for a work well done. We have gathered here this day to bid ourselves a prosperous farewell for having completed this part of our senior seminary formation. It is my and our prayer for God to bring out joy to a perfect end, amen.

As Heidegger would say, "man is a being in the world", this being in the world presupposes many things of which one of the most important of them is inter-relational. That is, man is called to live and survive in a community of fellow men, to live in harmony and sometimes in conflict with each other, to be of help to one another, to share with and to love one another. This fact of being in the world, as a sharer and giver, is the reason why we have come to you this day. Some might not understand the meaning of what we are doing, some might see it as irrelevant, others as unnecessary and so on. But I am very sure of one thing, and that is, the validity or the authenticity of what we are about to do does not lie in its discernment or acceptance by anybody, but in its ontology.

WHAT DOES IT MEAN TO BE WHAT YOU ARE?

Dear brothers, man as a being in the world cannot run away from being of help to and also being a receiver of help from the other. It is very much reciprocal and cannot but be a form of I-Thou relationship in the understanding of Martin Buber, unless one wants to be the Aristotelian beast characterized by solitude and loneliness. As far as we cannot be solely alone in the world, we are bound to enrich one another, and it is on this note of enrichment that we have come this day to thank, appreciate and at the same time conscientize you all to remain what you are.

From the above, a rigorous question runs into our minds, and that is, what does it mean to be what you are. From this another question might emerge on what the word 'being' means. We are not here to talk about the history of the speculative concept of being in Philosophy, neither are we here to teach the Philosophy of Being, rather, we have come to talk on a being that is more existential and practical. This is because the deriving force of this *tete-a-te* is a vividly, an astonishing achievement of a more practical orientation from which any relational engagement yields fruit in the person of the encounter. This reflection is titled "Being What You Are" because the deriving force is a result of your being, and being what you are. It is a result of your being because it flows from you with force and alacrity, with eagerness and simplicity, with ingenuity and creativity and most of all in the spirit of a being in the world that must survive along side with others. Being, with respect to this reflection, is strictly existential and of practical experience.

As Fr. Dr. C. C. Uzondu would say, "Being human is the primordial vocation of every human person", and for him, this vocation is continuous until death. Being human involves many things, which includes, being creative, and it is because of this aspect of being human, i.e. being creative, that we have come here this day. To thank you for your creativeness and invention by way of "Potential Leaders Forum' (FOLEF), an association of intellectual orientation founded by your class through the godly inspiration of Nzekwe Justin and his colleagues. It is the first of its kind in our institution. We appreciate it because it is an act of being in the world as we have understood it in this reflection. We are the beneficiaries of this noble association and cannot stop thanking God for your noble class, made up of inestimable characters of immeasurable creativity. Our promise here is that we shall do everything within our reach to preserve the integrity and the focus of the association to the greater glory of God and to our own benefit.

It is on this note that I wish to call to your mind the core theme of this reflection, that of being what you are. We are here today to thank you because of what you are and the goodies we have gained from your being what you are. To be what you are, as a human vocation, is very grandiose and requires a higher level of consciousness. It cuts across all areas of human existence and that is why it is an ontological category. It can be slightly synonymous with the Socratic self knowledge. It is in being what you are that you can survive. It involves bringing out those inescapable condiments of human existence, by way of being in the world for the success of the world as well as the self. In fact, a life subsumed in the struggle of being what you are is the most authentic and the most efficacious form of life to encounter. It is in this spirit of being authentic and efficacious that we call on you to be what you are. This call is both static and dynamic. It is static because there is a constant on which this vocation is accomplished and it is also dynamic because it is transitional and of different stages. To be what you are is an imperative, it excludes every bit of inhuman exigencies, and it excludes all forms of brutish exuberance and delinquencies. It involves being human, being the true image of a perfectible human personality. It involves acknowledgement of the fact that we as 'being' for others and that we depend on others for our existence. It involves using our talents and individual gifts for the development of the whole human community. It involves acting as human beings should act and living a life that is not detrimental to the good and welfare of others. It is a call, in the Christian sense of it, to imitate the creator who created us in his own image and likeness. It is a call to be free and responsible individuals aware of the limit of our freedom by the freedom of others. It is a call to an authentic personal identity. In fact, the fulcrum of our existence is being what we are'. As Fr. Dr. C.C. Uzondu would say, "being is the Ur ethos and if you are a Christian, be a Christian; if you are a student, be a student; if you are a seminarian, be a seminarian; if you are a priest, be a priest…" For him also, the heart of these calls to be, is to be human, thus, for him, "if you are a human being, be a human being." We call on you this day to be what you are. You are a human being, be human, you are a Christian, be

The Art of Oratory

Christian, you are a seminarian, be a seminarian and finally my dear brothers you are philosophers, be philosophers. Be the Platonic philosopher who is capable of ruling the state, be the Aristotelian philosopher who is capable of saying something about every topic. I want you to know this, from your being, which is being what you are, many people will draw their reason for living, many will be called to a greater life of perfection, many will hunger to see God, and even, many will hunger to be what you are now without your knowing it. So, I put it to you this day as an imperative to be what you are at every point in time and with this you will achieve even more than you have now. The reward of a thing well done is to have done it. So, continue in this act of being so that people may draw from the wealth of God's grace in you and may your being yield more fruit than the why of our here today.

Dear brothers, we love you all, we appreciate you all, we cherish you all, we care for you all and we pray for you all. We say and mean all these for you because of what you are. Being what you are, in this context, is a reminder and also a call. And because we have seen and have experienced what you are, we remind and call on you to remain and be what you are. At your places of long apostolic work, be what you are; for those who will come back immediately, be what you are as you come back; For those who may not like to continue in the seminary system, be what you are wherever you find yourself; and for all of us collectively, let us be what we are in all that we do. It is in being what we are that our existence is evidenced. We are authentic and mature when we remain in the realm of being what we are.

It is on this note that your immediate younger brothers say thank you; the executives of NAPS say thank you; the entire body of NAPS say thank you, and finally, the whole members of 'POLEF' say thank you. May the creator of the universe grant us the grace and the strength to be what we are to the greater glory of his name and for our own good. Thanks and God bless you all.

Appendix Four

The speech delivered by His Holiness Pope Francis on the 24th day of September 2015. He delivered it at the United States Capitol (Washington, D. C.), to the Joint Session of the United States Congress on his Apostolic Journey to the United States. This speech is popularly recognized with this title, 'I am Convinced That We Can Make A Difference'. Here is the full speech:

Mr. Vice-President,
Mr. Speaker,
Honourable Members of Congress,
Dear Friends,

I am most grateful for your invitation to address this Joint Session of Congress in "the land of the free and the home of the brave". I would like to think that the reason for this is that I too am a son of this great continent, from which we have all received so much and toward which we share a common responsibility.

Each son or daughter of a given country has a mission, a personal and social responsibility. Your own responsibility as members of Congress is to enable this country, by your legislative activity, to grow as a nation. You are the face of its people, their representatives. You are called to defend and preserve the dignity of your fellow citizens in the tireless and demanding pursuit of the common good, for this is the chief aim of all politics. A political society endures when it seeks, as a vocation, to satisfy common needs by stimulating the growth of all its members, especially those in situations of greater vulnerability or risk. Legislative activity is always based on care for the people. To this you have been invited, called and convened by those who elected you.

Yours is a work which makes me reflect in two ways on the figure of Moses. On the one hand, the patriarch and lawgiver of the people of Israel symbolizes the need of peoples to keep alive their sense of unity by means of just legislation. On the other, the figure of Moses leads us directly to God and thus to the transcendent dignity of the human being. Moses provides us with a good synthesis of your work: you are asked to protect, by means of the law, the image and likeness fashioned by God on every human face.

Today I would like not only to address you, but through you the entire people of the United States. Here, together with their representatives, I would like to take this opportunity to dialogue with the many thousands of men and women who strive each day to do an honest day's work, to bring home their daily bread, to save money and —one step at a time – to build a better life for their families. These are men and women who are not concerned simply with paying their taxes, but in their own quiet way sustain the life of society. They generate solidarity by their actions, and they create organizations which offer a helping hand to those most in need.

I would also like to enter into dialogue with the many elderly persons who are a storehouse of wisdom forged by experience, and who seek in many ways, especially through volunteer work, to share their stories and their insights. I know that many of them are retired, but still active; they keep working to build up this land. I also want to dialogue with all those young people who are working to realize their great and noble aspirations, who are not led astray by facile proposals, and who face difficult situations, often as a result of immaturity on the part of many adults. I wish to dialogue with all of you, and I would like to do so through the historical memory of your people.

My visit takes place at a time when men and women of good will are marking the anniversaries of several great Americans. The complexities of history and the reality of human weakness notwithstanding, these men and women, for all their many differences and limitations, were able by hard work and self-sacrifice – some at the cost of their lives – to build a better future. They shaped fundamental values which will endure forever in the spirit of the American people. A people with this spirit can live through many crises, tensions and conflicts, while always finding the resources to move forward, and to do so with dignity. These men and women offer us a way of seeing and interpreting reality. In honouring their memory, we are inspired, even amid conflicts, and in the here and now of each day, to draw upon our deepest cultural reserves.

I would like to mention four of these Americans: Abraham Lincoln, Martin Luther King, Dorothy Day and Thomas Merton.

This year marks the one hundred and fiftieth anniversary of the assassination of President Abraham Lincoln, the guardian of liberty, who laboured tirelessly that "this nation, under God, [might] have a new birth of freedom". Building a future of freedom requires love of the common good and cooperation in a spirit of subsidiarity and solidarity.

All of us are quite aware of, and deeply worried by, the disturbing social and political situation of the world today. Our world is increasingly a place of violent conflict, hatred and brutal atrocities, committed even in the name of God and of religion. We know that no religion is immune from forms of individual delusion or ideological extremism. This means that we must be especially attentive to every type of fundamentalism, whether religious or of any other kind. A delicate balance is required to combat violence perpetrated in the name of a religion, an ideology or an economic system, while also safeguarding religious freedom, intellectual freedom and individual freedoms. But there is another temptation which we must especially guard against: the simplistic reductionism which sees only good or evil; or, if you will, the righteous and sinners. The contemporary world, with its open wounds which affect so many of our brothers

and sisters, demands that we confront every form of polarization which would divide it into these two camps. We know that in the attempt to be freed of the enemy without, we can be tempted to feed the enemy within. To imitate the hatred and violence of tyrants and murderers is the best way to take their place. That is something which you, as a people, reject.

Our response must instead be one of hope and healing, of peace and justice. We are asked to summon the courage and the intelligence to resolve today's many geopolitical and economic crises. Even in the developed world, the effects of unjust structures and actions are all too apparent. Our efforts must aim at restoring hope, righting wrongs, maintaining commitments, and thus promoting the well-being of individuals and of peoples. We must move forward together, as one, in a renewed spirit of fraternity and solidarity, cooperating generously for the common good.

The challenges facing us today call for a renewal of that spirit of cooperation, which has accomplished so much good throughout the history of the United States. The complexity, the gravity and the urgency of these challenges demand that we pool our resources and talents, and resolve to support one another, with respect for our differences and our convictions of conscience.

In this land, the various religious denominations have greatly contributed to building and strengthening society. It is important that today, as in the past, the voice of faith continue to be heard, for it is a voice of fraternity and love, which tries to bring out the best in each person and in each society. Such cooperation is a powerful resource in the battle to eliminate new global forms of slavery, born of grave injustices which can be overcome only through new policies and new forms of social consensus.

Here I think of the political history of the United States, where democracy is deeply rooted in the mind of the American people. All political activity must serve and promote the good of the human person and be based on respect for his or her dignity. "We hold these truths to be self-evident, that all men are created equal, that they are endowed by their Creator with certain unalienable rights, that among these are life, liberty and the pursuit of happiness" (*Declaration of Independence*, 4 July 1776). If politics must truly be at the service of the human person, it follows that it cannot be a slave to the economy and finance. Politics is, instead, an expression of our compelling need to live as one, in order to build as one the greatest common good: that of a community which sacrifices particular interests in order to share, in justice and peace, its goods, its interests, its social life. I do not underestimate the difficulty that this involves, but I encourage you in this effort.

Here too I think of the march which Martin Luther King led from Selma to Montgomery fifty years ago as part of the campaign to fulfil his "dream" of full civil and political rights for African Americans. That dream continues to inspire us all. I am happy that America continues to be, for many, a land of "dreams". Dreams which lead to action, to participation, to commitment. Dreams which awaken what is deepest and truest in the life of a people.

In recent centuries, millions of people came to this land to pursue their dream of building a future in freedom. We, the people of this continent, are not fearful of foreigners, because most of us were once foreigners. I say this to you as the son of immigrants, knowing that so many of you are also descended from immigrants. Tragically, the rights of those

who were here long before us were not always respected. For those peoples and their nations, from the heart of American democracy, I wish to reaffirm my highest esteem and appreciation. Those first contacts were often turbulent and violent, but it is difficult to judge the past by the criteria of the present. Nonetheless, when the stranger in our midst appeals to us, we must not repeat the sins and the errors of the past. We must resolve now to live as nobly and as justly as possible, as we educate new generations not to turn their back on our "neighbours" and everything around us. Building a nation calls us to recognize that we must constantly relate to others, rejecting a mindset of hostility in order to adopt one of reciprocal subsidiarity, in a constant effort to do our best. I am confident that we can do this.

Our world is facing a refugee crisis of a magnitude not seen since the Second World War. This presents us with great challenges and many hard decisions. On this continent, too, thousands of persons are led to travel north in search of a better life for themselves and for their loved ones, in search of greater opportunities. Is this not what we want for our own children? We must not be taken aback by their numbers, but rather view them as persons, seeing their faces and listening to their stories, trying to respond as best we can to their situation. To respond in a way which is always humane, just and fraternal. We need to avoid a common temptation nowadays: to discard whatever proves troublesome. Let us remember the Golden Rule: "Do unto others as you would have them do unto you" (*Mt* 7:12).

This Rule points us in a clear direction. Let us treat others with the same passion and compassion with which we want to be treated. Let us seek for others the same possibilities which we seek for ourselves. Let us help others to grow, as we would like to be helped ourselves. In a word, if we want security, let us give security; if we want life, let us give life; if we want opportunities, let us provide opportunities. The yardstick we use for others will be the yardstick which time will use for us. The Golden Rule also reminds us of our responsibility to protect and defend human life at every stage of its development.

This conviction has led me, from the beginning of my ministry, to advocate at different levels for the global abolition of the death penalty. I am convinced that this way is the best, since every life is sacred, every human person is endowed with an inalienable dignity, and society can only benefit from the rehabilitation of those convicted of crimes. Recently my brother bishops here in the United States renewed their call for the abolition of the death penalty. Not only do I support them, but I also offer encouragement to all those who are convinced that a just and necessary punishment must never exclude the dimension of hope and the goal of rehabilitation.

In these times when social concerns are so important, I cannot fail to mention the Servant of God Dorothy Day, who founded the *Catholic Worker Movement*. Her social activism, her passion for justice and for the cause of the oppressed, were inspired by the Gospel, her faith, and the example of the saints.

How much progress has been made in this area in so many parts of the world! How much has been done in these first years of the third millennium to raise people out of extreme poverty! I know that you share my conviction that much more still needs to be done, and that in times of crisis and economic hardship a spirit of global solidarity must not be lost. At the same time I would encourage you to keep in mind all those people around us who are trapped in a cycle of poverty. They too need to be given hope. The fight against poverty and hunger must be fought constantly and on many fronts, especially in its causes. I know that many Americans today, as in the past, are working to deal with this problem.

It goes without saying that part of this great effort is the creation and distribution of wealth. The right use of natural resources, the proper application of technology and the harnessing of the spirit of enterprise are essential elements of an economy which seeks to be modern, inclusive and sustainable. "Business is a noble vocation, directed to producing wealth and improving the world. It can be a fruitful source of prosperity for the area in which it operates, especially if it sees the creation of jobs as an essential part of its service to the common good" (*Laudato Si'*, 129). This common good also includes the earth, a central theme of the encyclical which I recently wrote in order to "enter into dialogue with all people about our common home" (ibid., 3). "We need a conversation which includes everyone, since the environmental challenge we are undergoing, and its human roots, concern and affect us all" (ibid., 14).

In *Laudato Si'*, I call for a courageous and responsible effort to "redirect our steps" (ibid., 61), and to avert the most serious effects of the environmental deterioration caused by human activity. I am convinced that we can make a difference and I have no doubt that the United States – and this Congress – have an important role to play. Now is the time for courageous actions and strategies, aimed at implementing a "culture of care" (ibid., 231) and "an integrated approach to combating poverty, restoring dignity to the excluded, and at the same time protecting nature" (ibid., 139). "We have the freedom needed to limit and direct technology" (ibid., 112); "to devise intelligent ways of… developing and limiting our power" (ibid., 78); and to put technology "at the service of another type of progress, one which is healthier, more human, more social, more integral" (ibid., 112). In this regard, I am confident that America's outstanding academic and research institutions can make a vital contribution in the years ahead.

A century ago, at the beginning of the Great War, which Pope Benedict XV termed a "pointless slaughter", another notable American was born: the Cistercian monk Thomas Merton. He remains a source of spiritual inspiration and a guide for many people. In his autobiography he wrote: "I came into the world. Free by nature, in the image of God, I was nevertheless the prisoner of my own violence and my own selfishness, in the image of the world into which I was born. That world was the picture of Hell, full of men like myself, loving God, and yet hating him; born to love him, living instead in fear of hopeless self-contradictory hungers". Merton was above all a man of prayer, a thinker who challenged the certitudes of his time and opened new horizons for souls and for the Church. He was also a man of dialogue, a promoter of peace between peoples and religions.

The Art of Oratory

From this perspective of dialogue, I would like to recognize the efforts made in recent months to help overcome historic differences linked to painful episodes of the past. It is my duty to build bridges and to help all men and women, in any way possible, to do the same. When countries which have been at odds resume the path of dialogue – a dialogue which may have been interrupted for the most legitimate of reasons – new opportunities open up for all. This has required, and requires, courage and daring, which is not the same as irresponsibility. A good political leader is one who, with the interests of all in mind, seizes the moment in a spirit of openness and pragmatism. A good political leader always opts to initiate processes rather than possessing spaces (cf. *Evangelii Gaudium*, 222-223).

Being at the service of dialogue and peace also means being truly determined to minimize and, in the long term, to end the many armed conflicts throughout our world. Here we have to ask ourselves: Why are deadly weapons being sold to those who plan to inflict untold suffering on individuals and society? Sadly, the answer, as we all know, is simply for money: money that is drenched in blood, often innocent blood. In the face of this shameful and culpable silence, it is our duty to confront the problem and to stop the arms trade.

Three sons and a daughter of this land, four individuals and four dreams: Lincoln, liberty; Martin Luther King, liberty in plurality and non-exclusion; Dorothy Day, social justice and the rights of persons; and Thomas Merton, the capacity for dialogue and openness to God.

Four representatives of the American people.

I will end my visit to your country in Philadelphia, where I will take part in the World Meeting of Families. It is my wish that throughout my visit the family should be a recurrent theme. How essential the family has been to the building of this country! And how worthy it remains of our support and encouragement! Yet I cannot hide my concern for the family, which is threatened, perhaps as never before, from within and without. Fundamental relationships are being called into question, as is the very basis of marriage and the family. I can only reiterate the importance and, above all, the richness and the beauty of family life.

In particular, I would like to call attention to those family members who are the most vulnerable, the young. For many of them, a future filled with countless possibilities beckons, yet so many others seem disoriented and aimless, trapped in a hopeless maze of violence, abuse and despair. Their problems are our problems. We cannot avoid them. We need to face them together, to talk about them and to seek effective solutions rather than getting bogged down in discussions. At the risk of oversimplifying, we might say that we live in a culture which pressures young people not to start a family, because they lack possibilities for the future. Yet this same culture presents others with so many options that they too are dissuaded from starting a family.

A nation can be considered great when it defends liberty as Lincoln did, when it fosters a culture which enables people to "dream" of full rights for all their brothers and sisters, as Martin Luther King sought to do; when it strives for justice and the cause of the oppressed, as Dorothy Day did by her tireless work, the fruit of a faith which becomes dialogue and sows peace in the contemplative style of Thomas Merton.

In these remarks I have sought to present some of the richness of your cultural heritage, of the spirit of the American people. It is my desire that this spirit continue to develop and grow, so that as many young people as possible can inherit and dwell in a land which has inspired so many people to dream.

God bless America!

REFERENCES

CHAPTER ONE

[1] E. C. Igboanusi, *"Normative Media Ethics"*, Owerri: Edu-Edy publications, 2006.
[2] M. A. Ezugu, Principles and Practice of Communication in Administration and Business, Enugu: SGS IMT, 1999, p. 19.
[3] J. Maurus, The Art of Communicating Effectively, Mumbai: Better Yourself Books, 2005, p.26.
[4] B. C. Oberg, Interpersonal Communication, Colorado Springs: Religious Broadcasting Inc., 2003, p. 8
[5] S. E. Lucas, The Art of Public Speaking, New York: The MacGraw-Hill Companies, 1983, P. 19
[6] D. Litfin, *"Public speaking"*, Michigan: Baker Book House Company, 1992. P. 20.
[7] J. C. Pearson & P. E. Nelson, An Introduction to Human Communication, Chicago: Brown & Benchmark, 1997, p. 11.
[8] R. D. Rowley, "Communication Competence: The Essence of Aligning Action", 1999, **http://www.alignngation.com/comcomp.htrn**(access 28. 02. 2008)
[9] Ibid.
[10] Ibid.
[11] J. C. Pearson & P. E. Nelson, *op. cit.*, p. 345.

[12] D. Litfin, *op. cit.*
[13] E. Hall *"The silent Language"*, New York: Doubleday & company Inc., 1959.
[14] J.C. Pearson & P. E. Nelson, *op. cit.*, p. 14.
[15] M. A. Ezugu, *op. cit.*, p. 48
[16] Quintilian, Institutio Oratoria, trans. H. E. Butler, Cambridge: Harvard University Press, 1919, 4: 355
[17] D. Litfin, *op. cit.,* P. 29
[18] Ludwig Wittgenstein, Tractatus Logico-Philosophicus, trans. Frank O. Ramsey and C. K. Ogden, London: Kengan Paul, 1922
[19] U. S. Treasury Department, Internal Revenue Service. Effective Revenue Writing L. Prepared by Lucille R, Spurlock, and L. B. Dawson, Wash. D. C. Printing office, 1961, p. 171.

20 E. Gamer, "Seven Barriers to Great Communication", http://www.hodu.com/baniers.shtml(access 2.03. 2008)
21 St. Paul Communication, Daughters of St. Paul Social Communication Departments AMECEA and IMBISA, *Basic Human Communication"*, Vol. I, Kenya: Paulines Publication Africa, 1999, p. 35.
22 M. Hahn, "Overcoming Communication Barriers Between people", http://EzineArticJes.com/expert=MartinBalm (access 2. 03. 2008)
23 Ibid.

CHAPTER TWO

24 B. O. Eboh, *Living Issues in Ethics,* Nsukka: Afro-orbis publications limited, 2005, p. 3.
25 Robert Penn Warren, New York: Modern Rhetoric, Harcourt Brace & World, 1970, p. 264.
26 S. E. Lucas, The Art of Public Speaking, New York: The MacGraw-Hill Companies, 1983.
27 National Communication Association, *Ethics of communication,* https://teach.laneccedulkenz!userpagcs.html/thispage=68 (access 2.03. 2008)
28 Pope Benedict XVI, World Communications Day Message, May 2008, 4, in, Raph Madu, *The Role of Mass Medial in Evangelization,* Madueke, J., Ezeokana, J., Obiefuna, B., (eds.) Nigeria: Rex Charles and Patrick Ltd, 2008, p. 321.
29 Pontifical Council for Social Communications, *Ethics in Communications,* Nairobi: Pauline publication Africa, no. 13, p. 12.
30 S. E. Lucas, op. *cit.* p. 37.
31 S. E. Lucas, op. *cit.* p. 39.
32 Pontifical Council for Social Communications, *Op Cit.*, no. 16, p. 14.
33 S. E. Lucas, *op. cit.* p. 40.

CHAPTER THREE

34 N. Umunnakwe, *'Speech Writing and Delivery"* in Correctness and Style in the English Language Skills, (ed.) Polycarp Azoma Anyanwu, Owerri: Spring Publishers Ltd, 2004.
35 Ibid.
36 J. K. Nzerem, *"Better English for Universities and Colleges",* Owerri: Favoured House Concepts, 2004.
37 N. Umunnakwe, *op. cit.*

38 O. Otti, *"Communication Skill"*, Unpublished Note, 2006.

39 P. A. Osondu, *"The Descriptive Essay"* in Correctness and Style in the English Language Skills, (ed) Polycarp Azoma Anyanwu, Owerri: Spring Publishers Ltd. 2004.
40 http://www.tc.urnn.edu/jewe100l/CollegeWriting/STARTIModes.htm (access 28. 02. 2008)
41 Ibid.
42 J. K. Nzerem, *op. cit.*, p. 101.
43 C. Onuekwusi, *"The Argumentative Essay"* in Correctness and Style in the English Language Skills, (ed) Polycarp Azoma Anyanwu, Owerri: Spring Publishers Ltd. 2004.
44 http://www.tc.urnn.edu/jewelool/CollegeWriting/STARTIModes.htm
45 Robert Penn Warren, Modern Rhetoric (Third Edition), New York: Harcourt, Brace & World, 1970, p. 61

46 J. K. Nzerem *op. cit.*
47 N. Umunnakwe, op. cit.
48 D. Litfin, *"Public speaking"*, Michigan: Baker Book House Company, 1992.
49 Ibid., p. 137.
50 Ibid., p. 138.
51 J, K. Nzerem, *op. cit.*, p. 10.
52 S. E. Lucas, *"The Art of Public Speaking'*, New York: MacGraw-Hill Companies, Inc, 2004, p. 467.
53 W. Little II, W. Fowler and Jessie Coulson, The Shorter Oxford English Dictionary (ed) C. T. Onions, Walton Street: Oxford University press, p. 973.
54 Oxford Advanced Learners Dictionary, International Students Edition (8th Edition).
55 J. T. Gage, *"The Shape of Reason"* New York: Macmillan publishing company, J 987, p. 46.

56 Ibid., p. 46.

57 S. E. Lucas, *op. cit.*
58 B. Mondin, *Philosophical Anthropology"*, Bangalore: Theological publications in India, 2004

[59] G. Berkeley, *"Treatise on the Principles of Human Knowledge"*, in Battista Mondia, Philosophical Anthropology. Bangalore: *Theological publications in India,* 2004, p. 56.

[60] B. G. Nworgu, *"Educational Research"*, Ibadan: Wisdom publishers limited, 1991.
[61] Ibid., p. 23.

[62] Ibid., p. 81.
[63] Ibid., p. 94
[64] A. M. Tibbetts and Charlene Tibbetts', *"Strategies of Rhetoric with handbook"*, Illinois Scott, Foresman and company, 1987, p. 227.
[65] Ibid., p. 228.
[66] Ibid.
[67] Ibid.
[68] Ibid., p. 227.

CHAPTER FOUR

[69] J. A. Mourant, *"Formal Logic"*, New York: the Macmillan Company, 1963.
[70] Ibid.
[71] J. D. Carney & R. K. Scheer, *"Fundamentals of Logic"*, New York: The Macmillan Company, 1964.
[72] J. Obi-Okogbuo, *"Philosophy and Logic and Outline"*, Owerri: Assumpta Press. 1997, p. 104.
[73] J. A. Mourant, *op. cit.*
[74] I. M. Copi & C. Cohen, *"Introduction to Logic"*, New York: Macmillan Publishing Company, 1986.
[75] Cicero, *"De Oratore"*, II, trans. E. W. Sutton. Cambridge: Harvard University Press, 1976.

CHAPTER FIVE

[76] M. A. Ezugu, Principles and Practice of Communication in Administration and Business, Enugu: SGS IMT, 1999, p. 77.

Further Sources of Chapter Five
C. Hayes, English at Hand, New Jersey: Townsend Press, 1996.

B. Azar, Fundamentals of English Grammar (2nd ed.), New Jersey: Prentice Hall Regents, 1992.
D. Hacker, A writer's Reference, New York: St. Martin's Press Inc., 1989.

CHAPTER SIX

[77] R. Sherman, *"Sherman's 21 laws of Speaking"*, Edo State: Diamond Publishing House, 2001.
[78] Cicero, *"De Oratore"*, II, trans, E. W. Sutton, Cambridge: Harvard University Press, 1976.
[79] S. Alien, *"How to make a speech"*, Benin City: By Self-Improvement publishing, 1986, p. 51.
[80] Cicero. *Op. cit.*
[81] S. Allen, *op. cit.*
[82] Cicero. *Op. cit.*
[83] Cicero. *Op. cit.*
[84] University of Hawai'i Maui Community College Speech Department, **http://www.hawaii.edu/mauispeechlhtmIJpracticing Speeches.html** (access 20.08.07)

CHAPTER SEVEN

[85] New Catholic Encyclopedia, Vol. VIII., Palatine.III: Jack Heraty & Association, Inc, 1967.
[86] F. J. Sheen, *Treasure in Clay"*, Bangalore: Asian Trading Corporation, 1980, p. 55.
[87] You Can Improve Your Memory! in, *Awake,* Earth designed for life, published by the Jehovah's witness, February, 2009.
[88] Cicero, *De Oratore"*, II, trans, E. W. Sutton, Cambridge: Harvard University Press, 1976.
Lxxxvii, no. 355, p. 467.
[89] Ibid., no. 359, p. 471.
[90] Ibid.
[91] V. Okafor, "Psychology", Unpublished note, 2004.
[92] Ibid.
[93] A. P. Sperling, *"Psychology Made Simple",* London: William

Heinemann Ltd, 1972.
[94] Ibid.

CHAPTER EIGHT

[95] D. Litfin, *"Public speaking:,* Michigan: Baker Book House Company, 1992, p. 313.
[96] Ibid.
[97] Ibid.
[98] C. B. Uzomah, *"International Business and Management"*, Owerri: Nation-Wide Printers Ltd., 2002, p. 63.
[99] http//virtual.parkland.edu/kredmon/speech-delivery.htm (access 25.08.08)
[100] R. Sherman, *"Sherman's 21 laws of Speaking"*, Edo: Diamond Publishing House, 2001, p. 89.
[101] D. Litfin, *op. cit., p. 320.*
[102] V Ferraro and K. C. Palmer, *Speaking and Arguing: The Rhetoric of Peace and War",* http.//www.mtholyoke.edulacad/intrel/speech/delivery.htm. (access 25.08.08).
[103] R. Shannan, *op. cit.,* p. 90.
[104] D. Litfin, *op. cit.,* p. 322.
[105] D. Litfin, *op. cit.,* p. 321.
[106] R. Shennan, *op. cit.,* p. 86.
[107] V. Ferraro and K. C. Palmer, *op. cit.*
[108] J. Seamon & D. T. Kentick, *Psychology",* New Jersey: A Simon & Schuster Company Englewood cliffs, 1992, p. 247.
[109] **http://virtualparkland.edulkredmon/speech-delivery.htm**. (access 25.08.08)
[110] Ibid.
[111] Cicero, *"De Oratore",* II. Trans E. W. Sutton, Cambridge: Harvard University Press, 1976.
[112] Ibid.
[113] D. Litfin, *op. cit.,*p. 327.
[114] M. McKay, M. Davis & P. Fanning, How to Communicate, New York: MJF Books, 1983.
[115] Cicero, *op. cit.,* II, XXVI, No. 120, p. 85.
[116] V. Ferraro and K. C. Palmer, *op. cit.*
[117] Cicero, *op. cit.*, II. XXVI. No 121, p. 86.
[118] D. Litfin, *op. cit.,* p. 331.

CHAPTER NINE

[119] Cicero, *"De Oratore"*, II, trans E. W. Sutton, Cambridge; Harvard University Press, 1976, Lxxviii, no 318.
[120] Aristotle, *"Rhetoric"*3.14.9, trans. W. Rhys Roberts, New York; Random House, 1954.
[121] R Sherman, *"Sherman's 21 Laws of Speaking"*, Edo State Diamond Publishing House, 2001, p. 65.
[122] Ibid., p. 65.
[123] R. P. Warren, Modern Rhetoric (Third Edition), New York: Harcourt, Brace & World, 1970, p. 20
[124] R Sherman, *op. cit.,* p. 69.
[125] R. P. Warren, *op. cit.,* p. 23. (*The bracket is mine*)
[126] D. Litfin, *"Public Speaking"*, Michigan; Baker Book House Company, 1992.
[127] R. P. Warren, *op. cit.,* p. 4.
[128] F. J. Sheen *"Treasure in clay"*, Bangalore: Asian Trading Corporation, 2005.
[129] T. C. Opara, *The Voices of Great Minds"*, Vol. II, Owerri: Good Samaritan Press, 2001.
[130] R. P. Warren, *op. cit.,* p. 35
[131] V. Kumar, *"The World's greatest speeches"*, Benin City Mindex Press Limited, 2006.

CHAPTER TEN

[132] D. Litfin, *"Public Speaking,* Michigan: Baker Book House Company, 1992.
[133] Ibid., p. 62.
[134] Ibid., p. 63.
[135] R. B. Taylor, In Battista Mondin, Philosophical Anthropology, Bangalore: Theological Publications 2004.
[136] B. Mondin, *"Philosophical Anthropological"*, Bangalore: Theological Publications 2004.p. 146.
[137] C. B. Uzomah, *"International Business and Management"*, Owerri: Nation-Wyde Printers Ltd., 2002.

[138] D. Litfin, *op. cit.*
[139] C. B. Uzomah, *op. cit.*, p. 44.
[140] J. C. Nwokeocha, *"The Consciousness and the Psychology of Improved Human Behaviour Developing and Living the Psychology of Rightness"*, Enugu: Snaap Press Ltd., 2006, p. 43.
[141] P. G. Zimbard, *"Psychology and Life"*, America: Scott, Foreman and Company, 1985, p. 573.
[142] Ibid.
[143] Ibid.
[144] Ibid., p. 576.
[145] P. G. Zimbard, *op. cit.*, p. 574.
[146] P. S. J. O. Ezechukwu, *"Actualising your Possibilities"*, Imo State: Chimavin Production Ltd., 2002.
[147] A. H. Maslow, *"Towards a Psychology of Being"*, New York: D. Van Nostrand Company, 1968, p. 153.
[148] C. Anagwo *"Understanding Creativity and Self-actualization: A Psychological study of Abraham Maslow"*, Unpublished diploma Term Paper, Dept. of Philosophy, Seat of Wisdom Major Seminary, Ulakwo, Owerri, 2007.
[149] A. H. Maslow, *op. cit.*
[150] D. Litfin, *op. cit.*
[151] A. H. Maslow, *op. cit.*
[152] D. Litfin, *op. cit.*

CHAPTER EVEVEN

[153] D. Litfin, *"Public Speaking's,* Michigan: Baker Book House Company, 1992, p. 137
[154] Ibid., p. 137
[155] P. G. Zimbard, *"Psychology and Life"*, America: Scott, Foreman and Company, 1985, p. 580.
[156] Ibid., p. 583.
[157] Ibid., p. 583.
[158] Cicero, *"De Oratore"*, II, trans., E. W. Cambridge Harvard University Press, 1976, XX, No. 85, p. 261.
[159] Aristotle *"Rhetoric"*, trans., W. R. Roberts, ed., R. McKeon, The Basic Works of Aristotle, Bk. I. Ch. I, 1356a, 5, New York: Random House, Inc., 1941.
[160] Vijaya Kumar, *"The World's Greatest Speeches"*, Benin City: Mindex Press Limited, 2006.

[161] New Encyclopedia Britannica, Macropodia, vol. 6, New York: Helen Hemingway Benton Publisher, 1973.
[162] Aristotle, *op. cit.*, Bk II, Ch. I, 1378a 20.
[163] T. C. Opara *"The Voices of Great Minds"* Vol. II, Owerri: Good Samaritan Press, 2001.
[164] Aristotle, *op. cit.*, Bk II, Ch. 5, 1382a 25.
[165] Cicero, *op. cit.*, L1, No. 209.
[166] Aristotle, *op. cit.*, Bk II, Ch. 5, 1383a 5-10.
[167] Aristotle, *op. cit.*, Bk II, Ch. 8, 1386a 5-10.
[168] Cicero, *op. cit.*
[169] Cicero, *op. cit.*
[170] Aristotle, *op. cit.*, Bk II, Ch. 8, 1386a 30.
[171] Cicero, *op. cit.*, L1, No. 207.
[172] Cicero, *op. cit.*, LL No. 206 – 207.
[173] J. William, Pragmatism, Cambridge: Harvard University Press, 1975
[174] E. M. Ome and W. Amam, Philosophy and Logic for Everybody, Enugu: Institute for Development Studies, 2004.

CHAPTER TWELVE

[175] Christopher & J. Rath, How to use a vocal mike, Ottawa, Canada: 2001, ww.rath.ca (access 22.08.07)

CHAPTER THIRTEEN

[176] Aristotle, *"Rhetoric"*, 3.14.9, trans W. Rhys Roberts, New York: Random House, 1954.
[177] D. Litfin, *"Public Speaking"*, Michigan: Baker Book House Company, 1992, p. 254.
[178] R. Sherman, *"Sherman's 21 Laws of Speaking"*, Edo State: Diamond Publishing House 2001, p. 119.
[179] F. I. Sheen, *"Treasure in clay"*, Bangalore: Asian Trading Corporation, 2005, p. 58,
[180] D. Litfin, *op. cit.*, p. 254.
[181] R. Sherman, *op. cit., p. 119.*
[182] R. Sherman, *op. cit.*
[183] T. Anton, in R. Sherman, Sherman's 21 Laws of Speaking, Edo State:

Diamond Publishing House, 2001, p. 120.
[184] Ibid., p. 120.
[185] Ibid., p. 355.

REVIEWS

It is the crown of every library for it constitutes the *primus inter pares* among the books relied upon by men of oratoric splendour, lawyers, men of God, and leaders of thought among others. Read it!
- **Barrister Prof. J. O. L. Ezeala**, *Dean, Faculty of Law, Madonna University, Okija.*

A book on communication is a delicacy for our present society which is struggling with identity and the search for road map. The author has taken a bold step to research and bring out this work that I consider very timely.
- **Fr. Cyriacus Elelleh**, *Admin. Dean, Seat of Wisdom Seminary, Owerri.*

The Art of Oratory is educational and dwells more on public speaking. The author did a nice job on the book.... I recommend the book to other scholars and academicians.
- **Jane Amaefule**, *Lecturer, Federal Polytechnic, Nekede.*

The Art of Oratory is a well researched, lucid and interesting exploration of practical and engaging oral and written communication skills. Its incorporation of a wide range of speeches made by some of the world great orators makes it very enriching. An invigorating book.
- **Nonye Chinyere Ahumibe**, *Lecturer, Imo State University, Owerri.*

The book you are holding in your hands has done a splendid job of dealing clearly with the basic requirements for effective speech writing and delivery in a modern society. I strongly recommend it to all; both young students and those in the academia.
- **E. N. Ojiaku**, *Lecturer, Templegate Polytechnic, Aba.*

I finally appreciate and critically fall in line with the thought

pattern of the author in presenting to the world the necessary points that will be a guide to a wonderful and effective speech.
- **Fr. Ifi Felix**, *Editor, The Messenger Magazine*

It is a timeless legacy and will always remain a veritable goldmine of resource material for all researchers in the field of Rhetoric, Oratory, Public Speaking, Law, Mass Communication, English etc.
- **Ethelbert Obinna Umeh**, *Editor, The Hallmark Point Magazine.*

This work is simply a hand-out for anyone who has something to share through speech and its correlates, hence it is designed for everybody.
- **Fr. Okpaleke Paschal IK**, CCE, *Winning Ways Series.*

The author's simplicity in language and expression broadens the possible readers of this work and gives an average reader a sure way to understand issues herein expressed. Try it and see for yourself!
- **Fr. Stanislaus Chimezie Ukoha**, *Moderator, The Custos Magazine.*

Printed in the USA
CPSIA information can be obtained
at www.ICGtesting.com
LVHW010326170224
772067LV00002B/253